The Everyman Curler

Oh! The Stories We Could Tell

Rae Kujanpaa

Copyright © 2021 Rae Kujanpaa

All rights reserved

No part of this book may be reproduced, or stored in a retrieval system, or transmitted in any form or by any means, electronic, mechanical, photocopying, recording, or otherwise, without express written permission of the publisher.

ISBN-13: 9798703909768

Cover design by: Rae Kujanpaa
Library of Congress Control Number: 2018675309
Printed in the United States of America

CONTENTS

Title Page
Copyright
Foreword
Preface
THE FINAL   1
FIRST GAME   7
GROWING UP   18
HIGH SCHOOL   26
UNIVERSITY   40
LIFE, HELICOPTERS, AND PEOPLE   55
THE BRANDON CURLING CLUB   66
COMING HOME   84
GOING FOR IT   102
CATTLE   116
KEEP IT SIMPLE   126
WHAT NOW   133

UNDER THE KNIFE	141
OFF THE ICE	149
RIVALRIES	161
THE MCA	176
THE STATE OF THE GAME	183
THE EXPERIENCE	194
IN THE TWILIGHT	209
Acknowledgement	225

FOREWORD

Why would you go out on a minus 40 night with a minus 50 wind chill to go to the curling rink to play a late game knowing you're going to be well past midnight when you get home? The question has perplexed curlers' wives (and husbands) for generations. It is a legitimate question if you live in a town or city and the curling club is nearby.

Even more so, if you live somewhere on a farm in rural Manitoba and the trip to the rink means a half hour (or often longer) drive, in a car barely warmed up by the time you get there, alone on a barren highway crossing vast expanses of snow covered fields.

Most curlers could hardly explain it to themselves, let alone their spouses!

Rae Kujanpaa, truly the Everyman Curler of the title, describes his reasons for playing the game in a successful (by his definitions) curling career which he freely admits flowed between the third tier of players to the upper second tier with mere dreams of becoming part of the first tier, "the TV players - the elite."

In this very readable book, Rae reminds the curler of the sounds and smells of the rink, the feeling of making the shot that won the big game, the haunting feeling of that one end or even the one missed shot that changed history, and the feel of being so deep in the flow of the game that nothing else exists for that short, fleeting block of time.

And in layman's terms, with insights from a professional career spent in the mental health and addictions fields, he explains it all to the non-curlers in the lives of every "regular curler" who ever dreamed of drawing to the button to win the Brier or the Scotties.

Rae Kujanpaa is one of us, the everyman curlers. He was a pretty successful regular curler who admits "curling was something I did in addition to the really important things in life." He is comfortable with the fact this defines the difference between "us" and the elite curlers. He is comfortable that not letting curling become one of the really important things in his life was his decision to forego any real possibilty of that dream coming true.

Around the stories of games won and lost, he weaves his story of facing the challenges of life. He'd call it an ordinary life with ordinary decisions: a first chosen career which never materialized, a new and successful career in an unanticipated field and more career changes later in life, a return to a small rural community to take over the family farm, the challenges of raising a family.

Those were the really important things in life. And yet on a cold winter evening or for a weekend bonspiel, like all of us everyman curlers, he allowed the game to be the most important thing in his life for short periods of time.

If you played against or know Rae Kujanpaa, his book re-introduces him in a remarkable way. If you never met him, through this book you'll know him and you'll understand yourself or the curler in your life a little better.

Resby Coutts
Curling Writer/Broadcaster, Observer and Volunteer
(and one of the Everyman Curlers)

PREFACE

Everyman, as defined by Merriam Webster, is "the typical or ordinary person."

I am the Everyman Curler.

Many of my experiences in life and curling are typical and ordinary. I'm not an elite curler, although I wanted to be, and not a household name. That's not to say I haven't had some extraordinary moments along the way. Why does an Everyman curler get off his couch on a dark snowy evening, go to a curling rink that is barely warmer than the outdoors, and slide forty-four pound rocks down the ice? It's not a simple answer.

This memoir was written while the world was in the grips of a global pandemic. A good time to stay home and clean out the basement. I found a box under the basement stairs that I hadn't looked at in years. I blew the dust off the items inside. There were plaques, medals, crests, photos, and newspaper clippings - my curling history of nearly half a century.

These objects mean nothing to anybody in the world except me. Even for me, their value began to diminish the day after I received them, and I've promised my kids that when I pass from this earth that there will be a manageable amount of stuff for them to sort.

I picked up a crest, ran my thumb over the stitching, and a few memories trickled back. I remembered how I felt all those years ago when the experiences happened. It occurred to me that I have a box of worthless junk and in my mind, a vault overflowing with priceless memories.

Curling was the thread that ran through fifty years of my existence. Curling was there when my life happened. Maybe you have a box of things that remind you of your curling, or hockey, gymnastics, public speaking, or any number of other things. Perhaps you have a photo album full of pictures that capture the moment when you tried, succeeded, or failed. It's a permanent reminder of the moment you felt something strong enough to keep an object with the power to transport you back in time.

What follows is the story my keepsakes told me.

Rae Kujanpaa

THE FINAL

"It's hard to believe how worked up I can get over it
I'm right on the edge of my seat.
I get nervous. I start sweating
I'm watching curling."
Wayne Gretzky

Final game...tenth end...last shot. I would be the one to throw it. We were in the finals of the World Curling Tour's Dauphin Clinic Pharmacy Cash-spiel. It was our tenth game of the bonspiel. The field had included a former Brier champion and World Men's silver medalist. There was a team from the U.S. There was a touring Swiss team. Road-weary drudges from Alberta and Saskatchewan were there. And many of the World Curling Tour regulars from around Manitoba were there too, as usual.

Our opponent had a rock almost entirely in the four foot, guarded. It meant I only had one option for a shot. It was to slide a rock one hundred and twenty-six feet down the ice and hope it stopped in a circle with a radius of about 14 inches. I asked my third to put the broom down at the edge of the eight-foot circle, allowing for about 4 feet of curl. I started to make my way to the other end to throw the shot. I kept my routine. About ten feet past the hog line, I turned around to look at the situation. Did I have the correct amount of ice? Yes. Next, I took a mental snapshot of what I saw. In the periphery, I could see that the rink is packed with people upstairs and down. The glass walls separating the ice sheets from the downstairs lobby, and the lounge upstairs, contain faces - many, many faces. I refocus. Snapshot.

While sliding to the hack at the far end, I began to visualize what I had to do. It's a draw, a weight shot. I imagine how hard I need to kick out of the hack. I feel my sliding speed in my mind's eye and "see" myself extending my arm and releasing the rock at the correct pace.

If I make this shot, we win. There will be radio and newspaper interviews. The publisher of The Curler is in attendance. He'll have some questions and post his article online. The CKDM radio reporter, who has been providing live updates from the rink all day, will say in his final report that the home team has prevailed over a very good team from Saskatchewan in a hard-fought battle. The bonspiel sponsor will present us with first prize money printed on one of those oversize cheques. It'll be big enough for our whole team to stand behind while I hold a handshake with the sponsor. Long enough for the image to be captured forever. A volunteer will input the last real-time update on the world curling tour website. The most committed of curling fans will hit the refresh button one more time, revealing a count of one in the tenth end, next to the name Kujanpaa.

If I miss the shot, we lose. I'll shake the hands of our opponents and congratulate them on their victory. I'll tell them they played well and deserved the win. I'll put my gloves and slider into my curling bag, sling it over my shoulder and trudge toward the locker room. The physical and mental fatigue from ten games will descend instantly. It'll feel like extra weight, and all the aches and pains will reveal themselves. A teammate will pat my shoulder lightly and say, "Tough one, Skipper." Our team will change in silence. The winning team will restrain their joy, out of respect, until they're separated from us. Somewhere between curling shoes off and street clothes on, somebody will break the silence. "Well guys. That's not the outcome we hoped for, but I want to say thanks for the great weekend. We battled our asses off." We all say something. "Yeah, great. I always enjoy playing with you guys." "Don't be hard on yourself, Skipper. Losses are never just one shot. We all have a part in it." "Thanks man." We'll go upstairs for the prize presentations to accept the second-place money in a small business envelope. The sponsor will say something nice about us. Then we'll have a beer with the winning team. My jaw will be tight, but I'll force a smile and be pleasant. It will take all the strength I have not to slam my palm on the table and curse.

One should not think about the implications of winning or losing before one has to deliver the final shot, in the tenth end, of the last game of a world curling tour event. And I didn't.

I felt intensely focused as I settled into the hack to clean my rock and complete the rest of my pre-shot routine. There was something missing. The sound of curling is one of the things I love about the game. When six games are going on six sheets, there is a cacophony of sounds: the hollow roar of forty-four-pound granite rocks with cupped bottoms rumbling over coarsely pebbled ice, the call and answer of skips and shooters yelling urgent instruction, sweepers leaning heavily on their brooms making a scrape-the-windshield after a light frost sound. There are other sounds, too: strategy discussed in low tones, the sound of shoes and sliders gliding back to the throwing end, and a few curse words. All of this is contained in a rectangular building with metal walls and a metal roof - to ensure the maximum amplification of the sounds of curling.

But not in the finals. The usual sounds are missing. I love the sound of the finals most of all. It's quiet, and there's a tension in the cool air. We can hear the other team exhale, and they can hear us. The players are insulated from the scores of people in the rink by plates of glass. The sound from the crowd, as heard on the ice, is barely a murmur. No other games are going on, no sound. In the moment before you throw your final rock, everything is still and quiet. Sportsman-like opponents will remain motionless, even hold their breath, until the stone is on its way.

I look up at the broom. I see the breath of my sweepers in the frosty air. It's a bit cooler when there's only one sheet going. I'm not nervous. I'm in the zone. My senses are heightened. I feel the handle of the rock and push it slightly to unlock it from its sedentary friction. I lift my hips and draw the stone back. My left foot draws back too. I hear the crisp sound of my steel slider on ice. I push out with force, and the dull rumble of one rock fills the sound void. I'm now past the point of no return. I feel my sliding speed – check, direction - check, begin to extend right arm - check, initiate rotation - check, release - check. The shot is now literally, out of my hands. The delivery process takes about three seconds but feels longer when you're in the zone.

I feel a small wave of anxiety. It's not heavy! I speak sharply. "I think so." In other words, in my mind, "Get your thumbs out of your asses and sweep you bastards." My sweepers ignore me. They're veterans who know the thrower is always most likely to overreact to their own shot. Instead, they have a brief conversation, as if deciding whether to have cookies with their tea. "Looks good, I think" "yeah," "a little bit," "yeah let's go" And then they begin to sweep. They continue to reassess and communicate. "Easy, I think we're good" The rock glides a bit further. "Let's go."

They start sweeping again, moderately hard. I've been following behind, trying not to interfere, trying to trust. It's their rock now. I yell, "harder boys." It's not heavy!

They sweep harder. We've crossed the hog line. Fifteen feet to go, and it's not heavy. I yell encouragement. "You got it guys. Stay on it. You got it." They do stay on it. My rock - the last shot, in the last end, of the last game, comes to rest... on the button! It covers the pinhole. In the second it takes for the reality to sink in, I feel a wave that starts in my gut and builds into my chest. Endorphin, adrenaline, dopamine? I don't know what neurotransmitters were at work at that moment, but I felt an excited surge and a warm euphoria overtake my body and my brain. If there's a drug that gives a person that same feeling, I'd best not take it. I'd never stop.

I had just won my first World Curling Tour event. I was forty-nine years old.

FIRST GAME

"Sports teaches you about character. It teaches you to play by the rules, it teaches you to know what it feels like to win and lose-it teaches you about life."

Billie Jean King

Our teacher told my grade six class that we would be going down to the curling rink to try the game of curling. It happened in Rorketon, Manitoba, in 1971. I was ten years old.

My ears perked up. I looked around at my classmates. Inside my mind, I was screaming with excitement. "Did you hear that? Curling!" The looks on their faces told me they were much less enthusiastic about the idea than I was. I didn't get it. I hadn't played a game in my life, but I already loved curling.

My teacher asked the class if anybody had curled before. To my astonishment, several classmates put up their hands. The teacher said that those with their hands up would be the skips. This was the first of thousands of mildly disappointing moments curling would provide in my lifetime. I had watched curling.

I *knew* about skipping. I so badly wanted to be a skip. Next, he asked if anybody had watched curling before. My hand shot straight up with such force I'm sure my butt lifted a few inches off the seat of my desk. "Okay, those with your hands up will be the thirds." Yes! We would go to the rink in two days.

Two days later, I showed up with my Dad's "Blackjack," one of two corn broom brands sold at the local grocery store. Our class walked the three blocks to the rink and put on whatever clean shoes we had. Our teacher had the job of managing 24 kids on three sheets of ice. He attempted to maintain some semblance of control by coordinating all three sheets. He'd say. "Leads for the white handle team - get ready. Lead's for the white handle team throw." And the leads playing the white handles on all three sheets would throw. Then he'd organize the leads throwing black handles, and so it would go. When he got to the thirds, he said. "Thirds throwing black handles – get ready." He looked at the hack on sheet one – no third. "Where's the third for sheet one? Sheet one, where are you?" He turned and looked to the far end where I was standing beside the skip. He said, "It's your turn to throw. What are you doing down there?" With my serious ten-year-old voice, I said, "We're discussing the shot." The edges of my teacher's mouth curled up. He pointed to the throwing end, and off I went.

I don't remember if we won or if I came anywhere near making a shot. All that I clearly remember is that I was hooked.

Rorketon

Rorketon, Manitoba is a three-and-a-half hour drive northwest of Winnipeg, in the Parkland region. The flat landscape includes poplar forests, grasslands, and swamps. The fertile grain-producing land in the southern part of the municipality gives way to thin rocky soils just a few miles to the north. Bush covers most of the northern half.

Our farm was situated roughly halfway between Lake Dauphin to the southwest and Lake Manitoba to the northeast. Early memories include playing with my tractor in the dirt alongside our house. When I raised the toy front end loader, I made a screeching sound (steeeeve) just like the squealing hydraulics on my Dad's tractor. In the late evening, I could hear the cavalcade of tractors coming back to the yard after a long day on the hay field. I'd run out to meet them and hide behind a willow bush until they got closer. Then I'd jump out so I could steer the tractor back to the yard on my Dad's lap. I was only four. My Dad did not discourage the idea of running out to meet him, however, he instructed me not to hide. It would be better if he could see me in advance. I proudly led the parade of small haying tractors from my Dad's lap. The crew included a guy who seemed only to do mowing, one who did the raking, and a stack man. He stood on top of the haystack with a pitchfork while my Dad deposited hay with his front-end loader and hay sweep.

My grandmother was an immigrant who spoke only

Finnish. She lived with us and was my main care giver during the day, when mom was at work.

Until my brother was born, my ever-present companion was my dog, Hammer. My Finnish speaking grandmother suggested "Elmer," but when I tried to say it, it came out sounding like Hammer. There are pictures of Hammer and me posing and a shot of us napping in the grass, my head on his stomach. When the first of my two brothers was born, Grandma and I conspired again to name him. We agreed on Henru, but my parents overruled us and called him Bobby.

I was almost as fluent in Finnish as I was in English until I started school. Our small neighborhood of elderly Finnish immigrants seemed to enjoy it when I answered their questions and accepted their Halloween treats in Finnish. I remember looking upward through the eye holes of a ridiculous Halloween mask and seeing our neighbor in tears from laughing so hard, "Voy voy. Hahaha"

Mom is the second born of five extroverted sisters, a school teacher, and a descendant of illiterate Ukrainian immigrants. Her Dad was a progressive, in a time that that was dangerous and not fashionable. He was a greatest-Canadian-Tommy-Douglas-style prairie socialist. He was involved in the early days of the Canadian Wheat Board and National Farmer's Union. His brother served three terms in Ottawa for the CCF (Co-operative Commonwealth Federation). While McCarthyism was raging in the US, Canada had its own secret files and a program known as PROFUNC

(Prominent Functionaries of the Communist Party).

The Canadian government had secret files of suspected subversives that were distributed to RCMP detachments all over the country. Upon orders from Ottawa, all these alleged communists were to be rounded up and arrested. Mom remembers the RCMP searching their home for communist literature. While universal health care and old-age pensions are widely accepted now, those kinds of ideas could get you arrested in the fifties. My grandfather spent a lifetime making the vast distinction between social democracy and communism.

The Rink

My parents were curlers. If you grew up in Rorketon in the seventies, the odds were pretty good that your parents were curlers. So, I was a curling rink rat. The rink caretakers would yell: "Hey kids, quit running around the tables." That never worked. My mom said if I didn't stop running around the tables, I couldn't go to the rink. That did slow me down. I really liked going to the rink. All the other curling orphans were there too; their parents wrapped up in on-ice happenings. The rink smelled of endless burgers and onions. If you saved the foil wrapping from the burger, you could make a great hand hockey ball – until the caretaker interrupted or re-located the game. Later on, at about age eight or nine, I actually started watching curling.

I loved the game from the start. I loved that the rock

started on one line and gently curved into another line. I noticed the rock would curve right or left, depending on which way you rotated the handle. But it was the skips that intrigued me the most. My eight-year-old eyes could see that they were the ones in charge. They planned the shots and instructed their teammates on the role all were to play.

At home, I asked my parents about the things that weren't clear to me. I learned the difference between an in-turn and an out-turn before I ever threw a rock. My Dad had two well worn, hardcover books on the shelf. One was a textbook on veterinary medicine (he was a rancher), and the other was Ken Watson On Curling. It became an often-used reference book.

Grade seven couldn't come fast enough. In grade seven, you could sign up for round-robin curling with the high school kids. Ours was a K to 12 school, so there was lots of interaction between the big kids and little ones. The thought of playing with the big kids was exciting. In the fall of the school year, there would be a draft of sorts. Kids from grade seven to twelve would be sorted by their positions, and then the skips would choose their teammates when it was their turn to pick. Draft day is highly anticipated when you're in grade seven.

The teachers gave noon hour curlers extra time to complete a four end game. The noon bell rang right at 12, but curlers were allowed to leave at 11:45 to have time to walk to the rink and play. Our rink was a three sheeter, and with 12 – 15 teams entered, we only played once or twice a week.

In grade seven, I was still too small to lift a rock or slide. I'd pull the stone back and push with all my might, sliding forward a foot or two on my knee. But I was a full participant on the team. I tracked the wins and losses, inserted myself into the strategy, and must have driven my skip around the bend.

I got my first pair of curling shoes in grade eight. They were white Bauers. I would put them on to watch CBC Curling Classic on Saturday afternoons. I was fascinated by TV curlers. My impression was that what they were doing was a world away from the curling we did. I would drop into my Manitoba tuck on the carpet in front of the TV, while a Manitoban with a tuck delivery was visible on the screen.

I bought one of those thin Teflon slider kits and glued it onto my shoe. I still wasn't strong enough to lift a rock, but I was determined to slide. The rink in Rorketon was constructed four feet too short. To compensate, the ice maker would place the hack as near the backboard as possible. It meant you couldn't draw your foot back more than a few inches without jamming your heel on the backboard. We in Rorketon learned to use the backboard to our advantage. We'd raise our left heel when pulling back the foot, rest it on the backboard, and then thrust forward with power from both feet. The effect was like blasting out of starter blocks in track and field. You could generate all the speed and power you needed.

The no-lift delivery was still a couple of decades away. Everybody on CBC Curling Classic used a back-swing. One TV curler from Saskatchewan had a back-swing that took the rock above his shoulders before bringing it forward. So I had a back-swing too. The problem was, I was still not strong enough to do it properly. I'd pull the rock back, heave on the handle to elevate the rock over the hack, and bring it forward while kicking out of the starter blocks. I would bring the front edge of the rock down at too steep an angle and chip the ice every time I threw. By the end of the game, there would be a little crater in front of both hacks. As the teams were leaving the ice, the ice maker would be on his way out with a jug of hot water to make repairs. He was far more patient with me than he should have been. Once, he said, "Don't do that."

Brothers

I was sports-minded growing up. I have two brothers, and my parents provided a concrete basement cage that we willingly entered for endless hours. Half was unfinished, so we decorated it for them. On the concrete walls was a mosaic pattern of puck marks. There were two plywood-covered windows where once there had been glass. The paneled wall dividing the play area from the rest had gashes along the lowest part from my brother's skateboard. Two floor hockey nets were the area's focal points, accented by a scoreboard attached to the support beam.

My brothers, cousins, and friends had some epic games down there. Games would only pause long enough to have a snack or replace a broken light bulb. In later years, my parents told me that they could tell when a bulb had been broken, even if they didn't hear it shatter. The frenzied sounds of the game would come to an abrupt stop. A minute later, a special operative (the youngest kid was usually designated for the task) would quietly sneak up the stairs and make his way to the bathroom vanity, where the spare bulbs were kept. They could hear him sneaking back down the steps. Once the bulb was changed and the glass swept up, it was game on. And the noise instantly returned to full volume.

All that hockey could make a kid hungry and thirsty. Luckily, our mom kept frozen shortbread cookies in large ice cream pails in the freezer, and the cold room was stocked with 7up. Our family usually hosted several dinners during the Christmas season with family and neighbors. There were a few tense moments when our mom went to retrieve the Christmas baking and found empty ice cream containers and no 7up.

My Own Rink

My eyes popped open wide while looking through the Eaton's Christmas catalog. There it was. You could order a back yard curling game. It came with red and blue rocks and a plastic liner to flood your rink. Circles were imprinted on the plastic. I asked Santa for the set and waited in anticipation like the kid in Christmas Story waiting for his BB gun.

The curling set was pretty flimsy. The rocks were small and made of plastic, intended to be filled with water and frozen. The liner made for a very short rink and attempts to flood just damaged it. The solution was to move it to the basement. We discovered that the rocks slid quite well on the concrete floor if they had a bit of sand in them. We used crayons to color the rings of our "house." We noticed that as we played, the wax from the crayons became buffed and more slippery.

We turned the crayon to it's flat side to wax the whole sheet/floor and buffed it with rags. Next, we took the felt inserts out of our snowmobile boots and found that you could slide on the crayon waxed floor with them. So there it was. Indoor curling, in our basement, with sliding and all.

On the ice, I was getting stronger and beginning to make shots more consistently. I played in everything the school had to offer and began entering local bonspiels with friends. I entered the Rorketon Men's Bonspiel for the first time when I was 14 years old. This was the big one – the show. In my perception at the time, the Rorketon Men's was the fourth most significant event in the world. In order of ranking, it was; the Silver Broom, the Brier, CBC Curling Classic, and then the Rorketon Men's.

Teams came from far away places; Winnipegosis, Eddystone, Sifton, and even Dauphin. I entered with two cousins near my age and an uncle who wasn't a regular curler. We won one of the four games we played, and to this day, it's the only game I remember from that bonspiel – the opponent we beat and even which sheet on which it was played.

GROWING UP

"Nature is pleased with simplicity.
And nature is no dummy."
Isaac Newton

My upbringing was simple; not backward, not lacking, simple. It was a simpler time everywhere, but in Rorketon, the wheels of progress remained in low gear. Our school division, as defined by constituents' income, was the second poorest in the province. There were few resources. Understanding who I was as a curler has a lot to do with where I was from and how we, collectively, saw the world. Hindsight provides more clarity.

We were geographically isolated. Modern-day highway #276 to Ste. Rose was a gravel road when I was a kid. Some sections were barely passable after heavy rains. The shortest route to Dauphin was down the "Turkey Trail," part of which crossed a natural hay meadow.

Large combines were replacing threshing crews in

the south, but not here. My dad owned a threshing machine. Numerous neighbors and hired men would come with tractors and racks. At the age of eleven, I was hired (for fifteen cents an hour) to drive the tractors and racks alongside the rows of stooks (a stack of 6 to 10 sheaves of wheat or oats). The full-grown men would pitchfork the sheaves onto the rack. When their rack was full, they'd hop on their tractor and bring their load to the yard for threshing. I would then jump on the next tractor to help the next grown up. I got to drive a Ferguson, a Case, a McCormick, and an old hand clutched John Deere. I loved it.

I started steering tractors at three and driving them by myself at nine. It wasn't unusual. Most of my friends had the same experiences. I started raking hay at ten, operating the mower at eleven, and the front end loader at twelve. I imagined entering competitions with other father-son crews to see who could make a good haystack fastest.

Ski-Doos and Sweaty Underwear

I spent a lot of time on our snowmobile throughout our long winters. Sometimes, the school bus would drop us off at home early to beat an approaching storm. I'd get off the bus, hop on the Ski-doo, and take off to my neighbor's place to check a trap line with him.

My cousins lived fifteen miles away. We would follow the pioneer trails through the poplar bush and swamps to get there. They lived beside Lake Dauphin.

We'd skate until dark, eat supper, and go out again to play hockey in the headlights of the Ski-doos. I'd drive the Ski-doo home in my sweat-soaked long-johns. The headlights only illuminated the part of the path directly ahead. The trees provided a canopy over the trail. It gave the sensation of traveling through a tunnel with no end in sight. I always slept hard once I got home.

Pole Vaulting

My brothers and I grew up with a level of responsibility and independence that defied our age, and so did most of our friends. We had independence around the farm, and we had it in leisure. It made us resourceful. Both my brothers excelled at pole vaulting. Theirs is an example of the resourcefulness needed when you come from an area like ours. To get better, it's best to practice. But if you don't own a pole-vaulting pole, a stand, and a landing mat, what do you do? You build it.

Our dad offered counsel. He spoke of a neighbor who'd been a standout pole vaulter in country school days. In addition to being a good athlete, the secret was to cut the right kind of pole. It had to be a green poplar of a certain diameter. If it was too dry, it would be too stiff and could crack. A green poplar would have flex.

We placed nails into two more poplars that would serve as the stands and picked the thinnest, straightest crossbar that could be found. We had no landing mat. They learned how to land on their feet.

That's how they trained for hours on end, vaulting with a poplar pole over a bar on the edge of the bush, near where the disc and cultivator were parked. When my brother set his provincial junior record, a reporter from the Winnipeg Free Press asked him how far he jumped. Bob's quote: "Not very far, but pretty high." Marc topped that height as a high school senior and continued with pole vaulting into his first year university.

I decided we needed a soccer net when I was about twelve. Building materials were abundant in the bush around our yard. I cut a couple of goalposts and began cutting the limbs off of them. On one swing, the ax glanced off the log and into my foot. Luckily, the blade went between my second and third toes. Unluckily, it split my foot up the middle in a clean slice. My dad had just finished sharpening the ax a day earlier, preparing for his moose hunting trip. The foot healed, but I wrecked a good running shoe.

For us, growing up included a waxed curling floor in the basement, a basketball hoop on the wooden grain bin, homemade hockey nets, a football field, and a pole vaulting stand in the bush. I never finished the soccer net.

Sports Are For Kids

Since then, there's been a shift toward single-sport specialization. Canada lost a couple of hockey games to Russia in the late seventies. The worst thing about that was how sports organizations reacted. Starting with hockey, it was now considered important to identify kids with potential at an early age, then place them into high-performance streams, almost year-round.

Curling has done a version of that too. Kids who choose to play competitively gain access to higher-level coaching and high-performance training techniques. Kids who like curling but want to do it for fun are left behind. Gone are the days when a few schools could get together and run a high school bonspiel. If one school has a team with high-performance kids, other schools are no match for them.

It's a double-edged sword. Streamlining the best athletes into programs that make them even better does work. I would have loved some coaching when I was a kid. Any coaching, actually. I got none.

But there are draw-backs to single-sport specialization. Orthopedic and sport medicine doctors warn that repetitive motion required by many sports can cause stress resulting in overuse injuries. Multi-sport athletes allow for stress relief in different regions of the body. Playing a variety of sports help kids develop skills they might not have if they only play one sport at all the time and become better overall athletes. Most importantly, they may discover a love of sport for all the other things participation offers.

Who's behind single sport specialization? The short answer is parents, coaches, and sport organizations. Parents can fall into the trap of thinking they're not serving their kids' interests if they don't provide the most advanced opportunities. Without a single-sport focus, their kids might not make the pros/national team/a college scholarship. Coaches discourage multi-sport participation. Missing one practice to play another sport will result in time on the bench. Kids are often required to sign commitment contracts to their team and coach.

All sports are seeing participation numbers decline. Curling clubs wonder where all the kids are. Is there a place for the kid who's not particularly good at it? Is there room for the kid who plays many other sports and doesn't want to enter curling's high-performance stream? Where can you get into a pickup game of any sport? What happens when a kid is in the high-performance stream in a single sport but quits, or is cut, at the age of fourteen? What's left? Video games and online activity?

We're a culture that celebrates the winners. We pour everything into the few that can bring glory home for us all. There have been many books written about and by the champions. I admire them all. They deserve the accolades. But do we celebrate all the other athletes enough? Some of them tried just as hard but lost. The cold hard truth is that a tiny percentage of kids make it to an elite level. What should sports be about for those kids who don't, the large majority of kids?

I suggest it can be more about learning to function on a team. Employers seem to love hiring people who have played a team sport. It can be about fitness and health. Childhood obesity and type two diabetes are on the rise. I agree with the sixty minutes of physical exercise a day guideline.

The most important reason for all kids to participate is that it's fun. It can be fun even if you're not on the top line of the tier one team. The second wave of the pandemic forced city kids to live like rural kids. I saw reports that sales of backyard skating rink kits were through the roof. Fantastic! When my kids came along, we built a rink together every year. Our kids would be out there after school and three times a day on weekends.

Kids have the puck on their sticks for much longer in a backyard game of shinny than they would if they played on the fourth line of an organized game. They might not even touch the puck in an organized game. At home, they're forced to use their imagination. They'll invent games with each other and by themselves.

My parents' approach might have been as good as any. Theirs was supportive indifference. We were never discouraged from participating in any sport. Encouragement was barely a mild preference that we be involved in something healthy. Outcomes were never emphasized, although the wins were acknowledged.

The only lesson I can remember getting from my mom came when I was about six years old. She beat me in Yahtzee. I reacted very poorly to the loss, threatening never to play again. She calmly said: "You don't have to play Yahtzee with me again if you don't want to. But I am concerned about your outburst. If you want anybody to play a game with you, you have to know how to win and how to lose." Best lesson I ever got.

I don't think they ever saw me play a high school volleyball or basketball game. They saw a few curling games, being curlers themselves. They allowed me to use the Ski-doo or my dirt bike to get to practices. When I got my driver's license, I was allowed to use a vehicle and fill it with gas at the yard's bulk tank. This was in exchange for "being good," which I clearly understood to mean no drinking and driving. It was a deal that was easy to keep. I loved sports too much to jeopardize it all.

HIGH SCHOOL

"The Spirit of Sports: The spirit of sports gives each of us who participate an opportunity to be creative. Sports knows no sex, age, race, or religion. Sports gives us all the ability to test ourselves mentally, physically, and emotionally in a way no other aspect of life can. For many of us who struggle with "fitting in" or our identity – sports gives us our first face of confidence. That first bit of confidence can be a gateway to many other great things!"

Dan O'Brien

For me, high school was about sports and more sports. In a small school, you can often make the team in grade nine or ten. I played volleyball, basketball, badminton, fast-pitch, and curling, defending the honor of Rorketon School. In summer, I played with the community's adult fast-pitch team from the age of fifteen. I was the youngest, smallest, and fastest player on the team.

In winter, it was mostly hockey and curling.

Our farm was only two miles from Rorketon. When the school bus dropped me off, I'd grab a couple of rows of whatever cake was on the counter, then jump on our 340 Olympic Ski-doo and head right back to town. I'd play hockey on the outdoor rink with the town kids until dark. Our town didn't have organized hockey back then. It killed me. I would have loved to play in full equipment against teams with matching sweaters.

In hindsight, I'm glad I didn't. I might have become a single-sport athlete. I would have sacrificed the time and energy I put into curling. Curling got its share of my attention. It was the one game in town that mattered to anybody.

Going to a small-town school in the seventies was uncomplicated. If I had a spare, I'd ask the principal for the key to the gym storage. I'd get the floor hockey equipment out and organize a game with other wandering kids – unsupervised. The answer I got to most questions asked of the teachers was yes.

The Eye Patch

Grade eleven brought a highly-anticipated showdown. My curling team had qualified to represent our school in the divisional championships. My team got more excited as the big day approached.

I decided to play in a floor hockey game, part of a tournament that included adults, the night before. Unfortunately, I took a high stick on my left eye. Blood spewed off my face. Luckily, the stick had cut my eyelid and part of my eyebrow and didn't damage my vision. The gash was about three centimeters long and took a while to stop bleeding. More disappointing was that this was the end of the floor hockey game for me. It didn't occur to me that I might need stitches, and I really didn't want to show my parents, so I went to the pool hall and hung out.

When I got home, my usually supportive parents wondered how I could be so dumb for a smart kid. They said, correctly, that I should have come home so that they could take me to Ste. Rose to get stitched up. They inspected the gash. It had stopped bleeding, the cut seemed to be drying up, and the eyelid was swelling. It was probably too late to put stitches in now. We put a cover on it, and I went to bed.

When I awoke, my left eye was swollen shut. It looked awful. My parents were concerned about eye damage and thought they should take me to see a doctor. I assured them I could see perfectly fine until it became swollen shut. And besides, divisional curling was today. They asked how I could curl with an eye injury. I firmly stated that I still had one fully functioning eye on the right side of my face.

They let me go. I love them.

My dad had performed many veterinary procedures on his cows, so patching me up fell upon him. He started with antiseptic cream all over the area of the cut. Next, gauze covered the area. Then he placed tape over the whole thing, beginning over my right eye and extending below my left ear. Perfect.

My teammates were worried when they saw me. I repeated the still one good eye thing. Then our teacher/chaperon checked in. I again pleaded the case that I had one functioning eye. And so we were off to Winnipegosis to play divisionals.

We arrived in a snowstorm. I had taken my parka off in the car and just threw it over both shoulders rather than using the sleeves. We entered the rink. My third held the door open while I walked in, snow swirling, coat over my shoulders, and a full eye patch. I didn't plan a dramatic entrance, but it was. When a small-town curling rink door opens, everybody looks to see who it is. It was silent for a second before the audible buzz. "Who's that?" "I think it's their skip."

Our first game was against Ethelbert. My team was stronger, and I had very few challenging shots. With one eye, I could hit as well as ever. But I struggled with the draws. Having two functioning eyes provides depth perception. With only one eye open, I had trouble getting the feel of draw weight.

By the time we got to the final against Winnipegosis, my eyelid was feeling better. The cool rink air made the swelling go down, and I could now see a bit of light at the bottom. Near the middle of the game, I could open my eye a crack. I adjusted my eye patch upward slightly. If I tilted my head back, I could see to the end of the sheet with both eyes and get draw weight back. It was a heck of a game. We were tied up without the hammer in the last end. We managed to get a center guard up. With my last shot, I needed to make a heavy-draw-short-raise and roll. They had shot on the side of the four foot, and ours was just above and slightly nearer to center.

I tilted my head back until I could see through both eyes. I had to keep my shoulders more upright to keep the angle high enough to see the broom while sliding. I raised our rock onto theirs and rolled both the raised stone and the shooter onto the button, behind cover. Checkmate. The other team had no shot. It's over forty years since that shot, yet I can see it in my mind as clearly as then. I remember how the situation looked before I threw, the rock's path, and the outcome. And, of course - the feeling. That's the real reason a person remembers minute details and forgets large swaths of time. It's how you feel at that moment. I looked up toward the lobby and saw our principal's approving expression, himself an excellent curler. Curling is but a series of moments. Memories extracted from volumes of benign experiences.

In this moment, I made a shot and stood there with an eye swollen shut, receiving admiration from those in attendance. We received a small crest that said Duck Mountain Divisional Curling Champs. On the way home, a Queen song came on the radio. We turned it up, and the four of us sang loudly and proudly - We Are The Champions.

The Hogline

Every small town probably has a rival village just down the road. On the Canadian Sitcom Corner Gas, the fictional town of Dog River is rivaled by Wullerton. On the show, every time they say Wullerton, they turn their heads and spit. For Rorketon, that town was Winnipegosis. It doesn't matter that many people from these towns eventually marry each other. When it came to high school sports, the rivalry was intense.

Two things happened in the mid-seventies that changed the game in a big way for lots of people. One was the change to the hogline rule, and the other was the invention of the red brick slider. When I started curling, the rule was that you had to release the rock and stop your slide before the hogline. Many curlers released the rock just beyond the house so that there would be time to come to a complete stop before the hogline. The new rule still required release before the hogline but allowed a follow-through slide beyond the hogline.

Rule changes are always controversial. Purists argued that people would take liberties with the line and that it would be hard to police. They were right. Now we could come blasting out of the hack harder than ever. If the volume knob on your guitar amp has a ten on it, why would you ever set it to four? Long slides ruled.

Arnold Asham, the founder of Asham Curling Supplies, is from Kinasota, just south of Eddystone, Manitoba. Eddystone curlers had some of the first red brick sliders produced by Asham, and they introduced them to Rorketon. The red brick was so fast compared to the thin Teflon we'd been using. Now, not only did we not have to stop sliding at the hogline, but we also had a slider that was fast enough to follow the rock all the way down the ice. And so I did. My guitar amp had a ten on it, and I had a red brick slider.

Back to Winnipegosis. My legend had grown out there as only it could with no internet or Facebook and just two TV channels. This time there was a divisional mixed bonspiel, open entry. There would be more teams: more boys, girls, and teachers from all the schools. The rink would be packed.

The problems started with my very first game. My release point was now just inches before the hogline, and with my high-speed delivery, I would follow the rock, sliding nearly the same speed. From the lobby directly behind me, it looked like I wasn't releasing the rock at all. Winnipegosis lost its mind. After the game was over, competitors came up and made accusations, threats. There were complaints made to the teachers, talk of disqualification. A supervising teacher spoke to me. I assured him I was releasing the rock before the hog.

During my second game, the outrage grew stronger. I could see competitors complaining to the helpless looking teachers. Two people came from the lobby area out onto the ice to threaten me. Quit sliding over the hogline or else. I felt quite righteous in my position and didn't change a thing.

I went to the bathroom for my pregame pee before

the final. As I was washing up, a big guy started talking to me and blocked the path to the door. He grabbed me and pinned me against the wall with his massive forearm under my neck. He seemed not to know exactly what to say. He held his *I'm-serious* expression for a second and said, "Take it easy out there, eh?" He continued to hold me up by the neck and maintained the serious expression until I replied, "okay."

The game began, and I delivered rocks like somebody shot me out of a cannon. Winnipegosis, it's mind was lost and irretrievable. About two dozen people came from the lobby onto the ice surface to monitor me. The hogline had a scrum on either side of it. I took a quick glance at the teachers, who still looked bewildered. With the two scrums watching, I kicked out of the hack as hard as ever. This time when I released, I turned my hand flat about an inch over the handle and slid down the ice maintaining this position for about twenty feet. There was renewed outrage. I was a shit, I know. Hey, I was sixteen.

Ahh, Winnipegosis. Thanks for the moment.

Curling was starting to get easier. We were rarely losing around home anymore. My high school boys team consisted of hard-throwing farm boys. Garth and Randy were strong sweepers. The most common broom in Rorketon at that time was the Rinkrat. The Rinkrat was constructed with three spongy limbs covered in a coarse synthetic material. The old corn brooms had given way to synthetics. Our team used a broom called the Cat Mark 2. It was a wider single bat of sponge covered with a synthetic sock. When my teammates got in sync with those brooms, it was something to see and hear (they were terribly noisy).

My third and best buddy in high school was Bernie. He was a huge fan of Rush and had a Geddy Lee hair cut. He loved throwing curling rocks hard – very hard. He called them hay-makers. He'd surprise me regularly by throwing an uncalled for hay-maker. We made a deal. At least once per game, I'd call a hay-maker as long as he only threw hay-makers when called. It was a win-win deal. Whenever we needed a double or a peel, I'd yell HAY-MAKER and put the broom in the exact spot we wanted to hit (hay-makers don't have time to curl). Everybody on the other sheets would stop and watch Bernie's hay-maker smash into his target.

We were a pretty stylish bunch too. While Bernie had his Geddy Lee hair, mine was more like Keith Partridge. I cut my own bangs and let the rest grow. I had outgrown my white Bauer shoes and now had a pair of green ones with a matching sweater. My curling pants were a pair of blue and red checked bell bottoms, a style that had only recently arrived in Rorketon. Later, I acquired a pair of blue corduroy wide-legged pants. I liked them because there was a lot of room for my knee to bend into the low tuck. I wore those pants for far longer than I should have.

The radio was always on; in our house, in the car, and at the rink. The AM stations played a short rotation of all the hits. The songs D'yer Mak'er, The Joker, and Spiders & Snakes, still take me right back to the rink in Rorketon.

The City

That year, when I was sixteen, we decided to try our luck at the Christmas junior bonspiel in Winnipeg. There were something like 260 entries from all over Manitoba that year. On Christmas Day, our parents drove us to the Greyhound bus stop in Ste. Rose, and we headed to the bright lights of the city. This was quite ridiculous looking back on it. We were so bushed and naive that we didn't know we were bushed and naive.

Mom had gone to university at the U of M, so she suggested we curlers stay at the St. Regis hotel. She described it as a decent place with a good downtown location. I'm not sure of mom's idea of a decent place. We got off the bus at the depot on Portage Avenue at sunset.

Industrial arts had undergone some changes in our school division recently. As a result of this new progressive thinking, the boys were placed in sewing and the girls in sheet metal. While in sewing class, my team all decided to make shoe bags for our curling shoes. We sewed two rectangular pieces of cloth together and put a drawstring through one end.

We jumped off the bus, put our broom handles through the drawstrings of our shoe bags, threw them over our shoulders, and began walking down Portage

Avenue to the St. Regis. We probably looked more like we wanted to hitch a ride in a boxcar.

The St. Regis was fine. There were kids from other rural towns there too. We hung with the guys from Winnipegosis. Some guys from Flin Flon wanted to fight and got one of the Winnipegosis guys alone and got some licks in on him. After that, if anybody went into the hallway, we went in numbers. Rorketon and Winnipegosis, rivals at home, allies on the road.

I tried to wake my teammates up early to be alert for the game. I wanted them to do stretching warm-ups. I'd read that stretching could improve muscle performance by twenty percent. But no luck. A couple of them had drunk some beer the night before and weren't into stretching. I had still not discovered beer and was all about the curling. We went to the rink, and they warmed up the usual way – by taking a running start off the backboard and sliding as far as they could.

It was great curling in the different rinks around town. We played on some of the keenest ice I'd ever seen. We did well in some games, but mostly, we got schooled. Yet, nobody blew me away. I didn't see anything that wasn't attainable for us, too – if we worked on it.

The Big One

I was looking forward to the upcoming Rorketon Men's Bonspiel. It was still the fourth most important event in the world in my mind. Our team was winning everything at the high school level, so we were excited at the prospect of being able to compete with the men's teams.

There was bad news. A few members of the club's executive wanted to refuse entries from school-aged kids. Entries were rolling in from neighboring communities; Ste. Rose, Eddystone, Winnipegosis, Dauphin, and Rorketon ex-pats now living in Winnipeg. They argued that teams traveling that distance shouldn't have to play a bunch of kids when they got here. The out-of-towners were entitled to a proper game against adults. The debate continued in the days leading up to the bonspiel. A few people dared to say it was about my team and the adults afraid of being humiliated by my team.

A special meeting was called, and a motion was passed. They would accept our entry. There were fifty-six entries in total. To run a three-event bonspiel with fifty-six teams in a three-sheet rink would be challenging for the draw master. Starting Monday, there would be two draws per night through the week. On Friday, draws would go until 3 am, and the bonspiel would wrap up late Sunday evening. Exciting!

We played our first game on Tuesday and won easily. We had proven that we belonged in the field, now we could relax and have fun. I loved the atmosphere in the rink. Two hundred twenty-four curlers were coming and going, with their spouses and kids in tow. The hamburger grill ran non-stop. It was standing room only in the bar upstairs. The downstairs seating area had three-tiered bleachers with spectators for every draw. The results of every draw were reported to the Dauphin radio station - CKDM. It's no wonder I thought it was a big deal.

We won our second game, and then our third, getting off the ice at three am Saturday morning. Our fourth game was Saturday afternoon. The place was packed. In addition to curlers going on and off the ice, there were teams not scheduled to play and their spouses. Saturday evening was banquet and dance night, and people often arrived early to check out some of the curling. We won again, in front of a lot of curious eyes. We were now in the semi-finals to be played Sunday; one of four teams left in the first event.

Rorketon was renowned for its banquets. Only the best cuts of beef were served. There would be tubs of handmade pyrohy and halubchi. A Baba would say, "You know there are people who can't make pyrohy." Other Babas would shake their heads. The dance started after supper. There was always a live band. Two-thirds of the field was out of the bonspiel by now, so the party was on. The crowd that night would have been close to five hundred people.

The rink was packed when I arrived Sunday afternoon. A buzz had gone through the banquet the night before, about the kids who couldn't be beaten. Grown men that I hardly knew patted me on the back and said they'd come to watch me.

We had some advantages, looking back. Nobody played on Rorketon ice more than we did. Frost would warp the ice sheets. By February, each sheet had a pattern of shelves, dips, and ridges. I knew where all of them were, and if I had the broom in the right place, my teammates made everything. Some of the teams just couldn't get their heads around negative ice. Normally, an out-turn will curl from right to left. On negative ice, it moves left to right. That gets some people pretty twisted up.

We won the semi-final easily. Our tightest margin of victory to this point was four up. It would be a two and a half hour wait until the final. We would be playing the final against an out of town team. We were the home team, and the crowd would be ours. I had a hamburger and a Pepsi.

I took my practice slide before the final game, then turned and looked back at the home end. The downstairs bleachers were full. More people stood behind them, and still more stood on chairs behind those. The upstairs bar was packed. I could see our dads fielding questions. The whole rink smelled of hamburger grease, cigarette smoke, and stale beer from a week of crowded excesses.

The men from Eddystone were no match for us. We won 10-1. More grown men shook my hand. In their eyes, I could see respect, acceptance, and even envy. It was a pretty powerful experience.

UNIVERSITY

"Friendship First, Competition Second"
Yao Ming

The first time I ever saw Brandon University was when my parents dropped me off at the McMaster Hall Residence. I had two suitcases with me. One contained my curling trophies. How insecure do you have to be to bring your curling trophies? I had started grade school a year early, so I was just seventeen through most of my first year in university.

I also arrived with a significant dose of small-town inferiority complex. Somewhere deep in my psyche, I had the belief that the level of achievement you could attain was proportional to the size of the town from which you came. This was not a conscious belief, but I carried it nonetheless for far too long.

One day, a girl named Valerie walked into my room. She'd heard about my trophy collection. She looked at the trophies, then looked at me. Finally, she said, "I want to curl with you."

I could have been the inspiration for the character Napoleon Dynamite with my response. I said, "okay." My buddy Bernie had also enrolled at B.U. We got a fourth and entered the Brandon University fall bonspiel. All the B.U. Bonspiels were mixed.

I'd heard that there were around two thousand students at B.U. In Rorketon, three-quarters of the population were curlers. That meant that there would likely be about fifteen hundred at B.U. I wondered how they'd run it all off in one weekend. I was surprised that there were only 24 entries. My new mixed team was pretty good, and we won the bonspiel. Yet, I wondered where all the good curlers were. Maybe there was something else, something more significant where they chose to play.

The next B.U. Bonspiel was the prestigious Blue and Gold Bonspiel, named after the school's colors. Surely the good curlers would be out for this one. I was told, "This is the big one." There were more entries, and most of them were the same as the ones from the fall spiel. We won first place in this bonspiel too – very confusing.

I did very little curling over the next couple of years. I liked going to university and decided that if I was going to be allowed to stay, I should commit to it. I chose a major and buckled down. I got involved in student politics and loved living in residence. I became so immersed in student life; I barely thought about curling.

I often hear people say they have no regrets. Really? I have tons of regrets. I can accept that I made decisions in the context of the circumstances of the time and what I knew at that moment. But with the clarity of hindsight -regrets? Yeah.

One such regret is that I did not seek out competitive junior curling in Brandon. I was seventeen when I got there and had several years of eligibility. I would have benefited so much from some coaching and competition with the better players in my age group. My game was developmentally delayed because I didn't.

Riverview

I met a guy named Ross in a geology class. He started university later and was a little older than me. I learned later that he was from Flin Flon and had played in the British Consols, as the provincial men's championship was known back then. Macdonald tobacco was the title sponsor, and shortly after that, it became the Labatt Tankard. He approached me and said, "I've been asking around. I heard you're a good curler." I said, "I dunno."

Ross took charge and said we would be entering a team in a men's league at one of the three clubs in town. I had a couple of friends who curled, so Bill, Stan, Ross, and I entered a men's league at the Riverview Club.

I was the skip, but Ross was the leader of the team. Ross thought it was essential to sit down after every game and review every aspect of it. I had never heard of this. I remember Bill saying, "Why are we doing this? We won 11-5." Ross replied slowly, "Yes, but how did they get five points on us?"

A couple of games into the year, Ross looked straight at me and asked. "Have you ever played competitively?" I was not entirely sure what he meant by that, so I answered tentatively, "Yes." He asked me to list the events that I'd played. When I finished, he said, "My god! We gotta get this guy to a cash-spiel."

I had always had strong teams for the level of competition around me. My strategy was simple. If there was something to hit, I hit it. If I couldn't find anything to hit, I'd draw another one into the house. I rarely called a guard. This strategy had worked well. Now Ross had enrolled me in Strategy 101. He said he was entirely on board with hitting if we were up on the scoreboard, but that strategy would never beat the better teams if we got behind in a game. I was twenty years old and did not know you call center guards when you don't have the hammer and corners when you do.

Bill knew of a cash bonspiel in Lemberg Saskatchewan, near his home town of Abernethy. We hit the road for my first cash-spiel. It would be accurate to say, "I didn't know what I didn't know." I felt like I got batted around like a dead mouse.

Back at Riverview, things were going well. We won some games and I was learning from my tutorials. We had some problems beginning mid-season. One teammate had an injury, and for a variety of reasons, we couldn't ice a full team. We defaulted a bunch of games. One day a person from the club called to ask what the problem was. I told him we were down to two and hadn't been able to find spares. He said, "Finish out the year. I'll see if I can find some spares to help you out." He gave me two names, and they both signed on to finish the year with us.

Brent, in particular, turned out to be a pretty good curler. There were just a handful of games left, and we won them all. Somehow, that got us into the playoffs for the club championships. We won one game, another, and then another. We were in the finals for the club championship. A day before the final, I got a phone call. The executive had decided that my team was ineligible for the club championship because of the two spares. I would have to forfeit or play with my original teammates.

I immediately called Brent and told him the story. I told him I was going to tell them to shove it. He said, "You should know, this is about me. I have a bit of a history with those guys. They're doing this because of me." He continued. "You deserve to play in the final. Get your original team and go beat 'em." What I did next became another regret. Don't worry, I'll spare you the entire lifetime list of regrets. I said.

"Okay, Brent." and I called my original team. Neither had curled in six weeks, and one was still hobbled. I should have called the club and said, "my spares play, or you can shove that trophy..." I didn't.

We had a grudging low scoring battle. We lost. It was disappointing to lose because it always is; but I was more disappointed with myself for not doing more to defend my spares. I was a victim of my own ego. I thought, I'll beat you with this team, that team, or any team. But it was my spares that had gotten me to the final. A good skip understands that curling is a team game, and nobody... nobody has ever won a game by himself.

Wheat City

I got a call from Ed the next fall. I don't know how he got my name or how it happened. I do recall he had an entry at the Wheat City club and needed a couple of players. Stan and I signed up to play front end. Our third was a skinny guy named Dale. Ed was a bit older than us. He had a five-year-old son at home (who turned out to be the future skip of the top-ranked team in the world for a time). Ed was a veteran with competitive experience, and I learned a lot from him.

Push brooms were quickly replacing the corn brooms and Rinkrats. And people were figuring out how to throw with them. Ed had a creative solution. He tied a small chunk of rope to his belt loop, then slid the handle through the loop. He was affectionately known as Eddie Loopowich.

This was the first year I'd ever played second. I enjoyed it. Seeing the game from the front end taught me more about set up shots and building an end. Ed was happy to talk curling as long as we wanted to, so we picked his brain a lot. At the end of the season, Dale got an offer from one of the big guys at the Brandon Club and Stan graduated and moved away. Just as quickly as it formed, this team was done. I told Ed I wanted to give skipping another go. He gave me some good advice. "Go to the Brandon Curling Club. All the best curlers in town are there."

U.S.A

That same year, a rival came to me with an idea. He said. "Instead of us knocking heads with each other at these university bonspiels, why don't we team up and knock other people's heads." I still bug him that it was his head getting knocked, not mine.

Cindy joined us at third and Denny at lead. We entered the Blue and Gold. In the final, I needed to make a hit and roll behind cover to steal the win. We hadn't seen any hack weight shots thrown in that path, so I threw a risky normal weight hit and nailed it.

The Athletic Director was there to make the presentations. We received these huge ridiculous-looking cowboy hats with the emblems of various NFL teams. They didn't match. Stan especially, loved his powder blue Houston Oilers hat.

The Athletic Director said. "In addition to these

wonderful prizes... This team will represent Brandon University at the Mid West International University Games in St Paul/ Minneapolis, Minnesota..."

What did he just say! Our jaws dropped. The event organizers at the University of Minnesota had sent invitations to various midwest Canadian and American universities. Our Director had decided the winner of the Blue and Gold would be our rep but didn't tell anybody in advance. Wow.

Preparations for the trip came together fast. The university would provide us with a B.U. Bobcat team van that seated 14. Stan and Cindy got their class 4 licenses to do the driving. We were given an allowance for expenses. But best of all, they found us a set of vintage B.U. sweaters; blue and gold V-neck pullovers with the letters B.U. stylishly placed. Stan thought his cowboy hat matched well.

I met Brenda while at university. She had lopsided curly blonde hair. I had a great interest in doing well in Historical Geology because we'd decided to study together, and I courted her with homemade deer sausage. About a year later, we started talking about a future together. But before we could get married, we each had to satisfy one condition set by the other. I agreed to waltz with her at dances, and she committed to quit hooking her out-turns. We've both been substantively compliant since then.

I invited her to come on this trip to Minnesota because there were fourteen seats, after all. Three more friends joined us. We barreled down the road to Minnesota, team and booster club.

The St. Paul Curling Club was the site of the bonspiel. It's a majestic old rink that is a sister club to the Granite in Winnipeg. Upstairs, they had a fully stocked bar and beer on tap. An old cash register sat on the counter. The bar was self-serve and on the honor system. Help yourself and put your money in the cash register – beautiful.

They loved their curling down there. A personalized license plate on a car in the parking lot said "WE CURL." One person had a hollow handled push broom, acquired in Scotland, that could be filled with scotch. The ice maker showed us pictures of his wedding. Friends stood on either side of the ice sheet holding brooms above their heads to form an arch for the couple to march through. The ice maker and his bride exchanged vows on the hogline.

We had one loss going into the last day of the competition. There were three teams left with a chance to win. They were; Lakehead (Thunder Bay), the University of Manitoba, and us. All the American teams were out of the running. We had games left with Lakehead and the U of M. We needed to win both to force a playoff. We won the first game of the day against Lakehead.

We had somehow endeared ourselves to the Americans. They were solidly in our corner. Maybe it was the entertainment we provided on the ice, or more likely, the entertainment provided by our traveling booster club. They had won a door prize of lime vodka and decided that no lime vodka should leave the rink that day. In previous days, we had accepted invitations to their homes, ate chili with them, and talked curling. We talked about the equipment we had, not seen by them before, like the red brick slider. It was strange to me that at that moment, we were representing Canadian curling in their eyes.

On the second last day, we sat with a large group of Americans upstairs, sharing a pint. Our favorite show on T.V. at home was the comedy SCTV. A booster club member and I slipped into character: we were Bob and Doug McKenzie. The Americans wondered what we were doing. It was explained very carefully. "You see. Rae here. He's a hoser... Brenda over there. She's his hosebag." The gasps were audible. "Did you hear what he called her?" My friend, sensing that something was wrong, leaned over to me and whispered. "I think hosebag means something different down here than it does back home." I leaned toward him and whispered back. "Actually, Bud, it means about the same thing in both countries."

"Oh."

Our last game was with the U of M. They were undefeated, and we needed to beat them to force a playoff with them. We got behind early but battled back and won. Now we both had one loss, and there would be a playoff to determine the winner.

Our booster club was excited and saturated with

lime vodka. A sizable crowd had assembled to cheer us on. Many people approached us to wish us well. During the course of the competition, the U of M team had come across as aloof. They didn't take the time to mix in with their hosts. Or maybe the fans just needed a good guy and a bad guy. I crossed paths with the skip from that U of M team several times in subsequent years. I thought he was a real good guy. Deserved or not, on that day, they were the bad guys.

In the first end of the sudden death final, with the crowd on our side, we gave up a four. Being down by four points after one end, it was hard to make ourselves believe it wasn't over already. The team was reeling. We tried but just couldn't get much going. This game was a decade before the free guard zone rule, so they hit everything. There was a glimmer of hope in the sixth end. We were laying one on the left side of the house. They had second shot in the back eight on the other side. And we had third shot rock in the top twelve, directly in front of it.

This kind of situation is why people like to watch curling. A fan can put himself in the shoes of the players. There are always discussions behind the glass. "What would you do?" Somebody says what they would do, and somebody else would say he'd make the other choice. They'll sip their beers and debate the pros and cons.

We had a team discussion. The simple shot was to draw in a second counter to score two. The other option was to play the raise on our rock onto theirs to count three. But it's a high-risk option, and a miss would mean a count of just one. The thing that solidified the decision was the scoreboard. We were still three points down, and time was running out. We chose the raise and made it. Game tied.

Momentum is hard to stop. Most people would say they'd rather be four up than four down after one end. But being four down meant we would throw lots of draws, and they would throw lots of hits. And the last end often comes down to a draw shot. Being four down frees you psychologically. You've got nothing to lose when you've already lost, and nobody expects you to win. When you try to hold a big lead, you might play too defensively. You might feel more anxious, even if you still have the advantage.

The last end came down to two draws. When I came to throw my last shot, we had a center guard, and they had one back button. It was an ideal situation for us. We didn't have the last rock and needed to steal the winning point. I released the rock on a good line. Stan and Denny swept. I yelled. The booster club drank. My rock came to rest on the button, in front of theirs. But it had over curled by about two inches. I had shot rock, but the pinhole was showing. The U of M skip threw the last rock of the bonspiel. His weight looked good. The sweepers were on and off. He had perfect tee line weight. But it didn't curl quite far enough and came to rest on the side of the button. We had shot rock. We won. We were the Can/Am Mid West Universities Champions. What a time we had down there.

The Quill, the B.U. student newspaper, printed the news of our triumph. I was named B.U. Bobcat athlete of the week. Our Bobcat basketball team was ranked number one in the country in CIS rankings. The hockey team was also in the top ten in the country. Some of my friends thought it was hilarious that I was chosen out of that company. Many had never seen me throw a curling rock. I got all kinds of ribbing. The athlete of the week honor came with a gift certificate to the Keg. I took Brenda. It was nice to get away from a student's budget for one night.

Our team was invited to the end of year sports awards banquet for B.U. Athletics. The Athletic Director made a compliment-filled speech about our achievement and presented us with medals. It was a memorable evening in the company of such awe-inspiring athletes on other teams.

The '82 Brier

The Brier came to Brandon in 1982 as well. I volunteered to be on the ice crew. We'd wipe down the handles between games and run the sheepskin over the sheet before games and at the fifth end break. I watched intently the rest of the time. This was the first time I'd seen "T.V. curlers" live. The attendance numbers were huge in Brandon. The whole event was a curling spectacle, the likes of which I'd never imagined. Brandon introduced "the Brier Patch" too, which is basically a saloon installed in the biggest room the host venue has. The patch is a phenomenon that continues to the present day.

What I observed on the ice surprised me. Most of the teams looked...ordinary. Curling, unlike most sports, is a game that looks better on T.V. The cameras frame the deliveries perfectly, leaving the impression that the players never miss the broom. Other camera angles give you the best view of the house, the rock approaching, close-ups, and replays. Commentators add drama to what is really two teams throwing alternating colors. I was surprised that the T.V. curlers were as ordinary as they were.

I was also a bit taken by all the off-ice shenanigans. I was in my fourth year at university. A party was not unfamiliar to me. Naive me thought that Brier players probably didn't drink the night before games. I was wrong. For an excellent account of this legendary Canadian sporting event, check out "'The Brier' The History of Canada's Most Celebrated Curling Championship" by Bob Weeks.

There were only three teams that I thought had any shot at winning the 1982 Brier. And among all the ordinary players, there was one exceptional team. They stood out above everybody else. Al Hackner, the "Ice Man," won the Brier and went on to win the first of his two world championships. As part of the ice crew, I managed to linger at the back of a sheet a bit longer. I watched the Ice Man slide directly toward me, then release the rock straight and pure. It was impressive, but not magic.

I couldn't have imagined that a few years later, I would play against the Ice Man.

LIFE, HELICOPTERS, AND PEOPLE

"If life were predictable, it would cease to be life and be without flavor."
Eleanor Roosevelt

I had my life all figured out at the age of twenty-one. It's nice, really, to have your life figured out at twenty-one. With all the major decisions made, one just needs to go about living. Just let it all unfold.

I didn't understand what university was all about when I enrolled after high school. I was interested in many subjects but couldn't connect the dots between something like History and future employment.

I was strong in the sciences in high school, so I applied to the faculty of science, majoring in geology. I picked the most practical program that the university offered. In the end, I would be a geologist. I liked it, an applied science that used math, physics, and chemistry at its core.

Life as a hard rock geologist could be an adventure. It was part of the appeal for me. I spent a summer exploring northeast Saskatchewan for precious metals. We tromped through the bush in a grid pattern, collecting soil samples to be assayed for trace amounts of metal. To collect samples from the bottoms of lakes and swamps, we used a helicopter.

The stocky, bearded, gnome-like pilot landed on a pad we'd cleared for him. He brought a toothpick shaped engineer with him. They landed in an old Bell 47 helicopter with a clear plexiglass bubble – think of the helicopters on the old sitcom M.A.S.H. The engineer replaced the foot rails with floats for landing on lakes. We joined the pilot and engineer for an orientation before we began.

The machine only had enough fuel for a flying time of two hours, no reserve tank. While refueling, the engineer would re-tighten all the bolts on the frame. Vibrations sometimes caused them to work loose. The pilot explained that to speed up the gathering of samples, his assistant would remove the door on my side. He was competing for contracts with companies that were using the newer turbine-powered Jet Ranger helicopters. To compete, he had to take a few shortcuts and fly aggressively.

We worked in alternating two-person crews, one navigator and one sampler. As the sampler, my job was to jump out onto the float and drop a twenty-four-inch cylinder down to the bottom of the lake. The cylinder had a butterfly valve at the bottom that opened when going down and closed when I pulled it up. We attached the rope to a strut on the chopper, and I'd reel it up, hand over hand, then deposit its contents into a sample bag held open by the navigator. The navigator would mark the sample and indicate its correct location on the map. We did this over and over, as many times as we could in two hours. I was often still standing on the float when the pilot lifted off to the next spot. That was fine. The only thing that made me nervous was when he banked to my side, with the door off, and my seat belt not yet on.

Bell 47s didn't have much power. They weren't very capable of lifting straight up. To get going, the pilot had to rotate the joystick in small circles to get it to lift a few feet off the surface. Then he'd tilt the nose of the chopper downward to generate forward speed before pulling back on the stick and getting lift. That was fine on a big lake, but we took some of the samples in pothole swamps surrounded by bush. He'd taxi up close to one edge, point the nose to the other side, and go, hoping to get enough lift to clear the bush on the other side. We trimmed the tops of a few spindly poplars.

One day, crisis. The navigator pushed the map toward me, "Where are we?" I didn't know. I was solely focused on retrieving samples as fast as possible, then catching my breath before again reeling in a cylinder that seemed to double in weight after two hours. The pilot didn't know either. He relied on the navigator to give him bearings from one sample site to the next. We were running low on fuel. We knew east from west; we just didn't know if we were north or south of our camp. Guessing wrong could be tragic.

The pilot decided to elevate. He wore a serious expression on his face. Maybe, from a higher vantage point, we could recognize a landscape feature that matched the map. We couldn't. Everything looked the same. Then we noticed something floating on the lake, not far from where we were. The pilot dived toward the boat to get there as quickly as possible. He landed near them. It was a couple of Indigenous fishers. The pilot taxied toward their boat. I jumped onto the float with my map and handed it to them. One of them put a finger on a spot on the map. I nodded and yelled a loud "Thanks" above the roar of the rotor. I jumped back into the chopper and yelled, "South! We gotta go south!"

Wake-boarding

The summer evenings are very long in the far north. In June, the sun would just skim below the horizon for an hour, but it was never dark. I put my farm boy ingenuity into action by building what is now known as a wake-board (no such thing in the eighties). We found an abandoned diamond drilling site that hadn't been adequately cleaned. While cleaning it up, I salvaged some materials; a piece of plywood, a stovepipe, and a tin butter can. I halved the stove pipe and attached it to the front of the small plywood, then flattened the butter can sideways to serve as a keel. Our zodiacs didn't have much power. I floated in the water with the board against my chest until I was planing. I made my way onto my knees, and eventually, my feet, wake-boarding on a lake in the middle of nowhere.

A few weeks later, it was time for our camp to move. We were being redeployed even farther north, near Lake Athabasca, on the fifty-ninth degree of latitude. I put up a fight when the Otter pilot told me I couldn't take my wake-board with me. I lost. He said, "If we have a rough landing, that thing might decapitate somebody."

One person on our crew was a water skier who had no interest in my stove pipe plywood wakeboard. Somehow, she managed to get her water ski sent to her on a supply shipment. It was a single slalom ski. We had a slightly more powerful boat at our new camp, but it wasn't enough to pull me out of the water with just one ski.

Core boxes are containers that keep core produced by diamond drilling in hard rock. They're about six inches wide and four feet long. I nailed an old running shoe onto one, laces out. I would wear the water ski on one foot and the core box ski on the other. Once I was on the surface of the water, I'd drop the core box and proceed just on the slalom ski.

Our assignment in this area was just three weeks, so rather than flying our whole camp up, we were housed in a remote fly-in fishing camp and helicoptered to work each day. A Texas oil company flew all its executives out to this camp for an adventure retreat. It was a long way up north, and the water was cold. One evening, the Texans got brave after drinking enough courage and dipped their toes in the water. They took turns running in as far as they dared, almost up to their knees, and squealing like children. They looked up to see a motorboat coming around the point. Behind it, me, on a water ski. I wore my northern wet suit; blue Adidas shorts over long johns and a yellow t-shirt. I smiled and waved at their hanging jaws.

The Opportunity

In 1981, I was hired by the Manitoba government's Minerals and Mines Branch as a summer student. We were deployed to northern Manitoba to map geology in the nickel belt. Our crew chief would present our findings to the mining industry later in the fall. We were a crew of six camped on an island for thirteen weeks. We went to work on Zodiac boats and mapped shoreline geology. We fried Klik on tin plates and boiled some of our meals in foil-wrapped pouches for lunch.

The only other people we saw on the lake were a small crew from the mining company Inco. They were also exploring the significance of the geologic formations that seemed to be coming together on this lake. The chief exploration geologist for Inco was a guy named Dave. I hit it off great with him. Occasionally, our crews needed to go to Thompson for a supply run. When in Thompson, I went to Dave's house and met his family. We golfed together and talked about me joining the Inco geology department when I graduated.

It was an excellent time to be a geologist. An article in the Winnipeg Free Press careers section said that each graduating geology student picked from an average of six job offers. I knew I could live on five thousand a year as a student. When I looked at what a geologist made, it was wealth beyond my comprehension. I knew nothing about the stock market but decided I could invest at least half my salary and let the market make me richer.

I breezed through my fourth year and couldn't wait to graduate and get on with it. Our class was a bit nervous. The economy was entering a recession, and there might not be as many jobs. But I had Dave. Inco posted two positions for their geology department to support a mine expansion that they were planning. I got an interview, and Dave was on the panel. The interview went well. The way they talked, it felt like I was getting an early orientation to the job: "You'll be doing this and in charge of that." I couldn't wait for the call offering me the job. Two agonizing days passed, and I heard nothing. I picked up a newspaper and flipped through the business section. I saw the word Inco in the headline.

The C.E.O. of Inco announced a hiring freeze. He

explained that the hiring freeze extended to all divisions and departments. The company placed its expansion plans on hiatus. And my life plan balloon popped, just like that.

Recessions Suck

The recession of the early 1980s was brutal. Interest rates at the banks were over twenty percent. There were large numbers of home foreclosures in Calgary, worst hit by the recession. Mineral and oil exploration ground to a halt. Companies laid off geologists with ten years of experience. The summer after I graduated with my science degree, I painted houses. That fall, when the painting was done, I was unemployed. My unemployment benefits were one hundred dollars a week.

My lowest point may have been when the manager at K.F.C. rejected my application. He looked at it and said: "Science degree? I can't hire you. You won't stay." He was right, of course, but I needed to work so badly I tried to convince him of how hard I'd work while I was there. No go.

A university buddy was in the same boat. We'd drink coffee and skate at an outdoor rink. At one pm, we'd go to the Brandon Sun building to get the first newspapers off the press so that we could be first to respond to any new job ads. This ritual went on for four months.

B.M.H.C.

A social worker friend suggested I apply at the Brandon Mental Health Centre (B.M.H.C.). I had so many job applications rejected by then I was running out of fight. I pointed out that I had absolutely no relevant educational experience. He said there was a program run by a director who wanted to hire people with no relevant training. That sounded unlikely to me. But I applied, interviewed, and got the job.

That director at B.M.H.C. gave me one of the best compliments I've ever received. She said she wanted to hire "normal" people. Thank you very much. What she meant was; people with no training in psych nursing, psychology, and other related areas of study. She postulated that people with that kind of background might be more inclined to see the mental illness too prominently, and "normal" people might be more inclined just to see the person.

B.M.H.C. hired me into a community re-integration program. Patients whose illnesses were stabilized and manageable could come to the program to have life skills assessed. Program participants practiced skill-building exercises, and eventually, they re-entered the community. It was a positive and hopeful program.

It was a life-changing experience to work there. I was a fit, healthy twenty-two-year-old working in an environment full of emotional pain. I was, until then, entirely oblivious to this kind of suffering. I hadn't understood how fragile the human condition could be. It was humbling. Overall, it was a humbling year. I had gone from having life figured out to unemployment and rejection, and now I was surrounded by hundreds of people in some form of distress.

What surprised this farm boy geologist was how much I enjoyed working there. After overcoming some initial fear and doubt, I began to connect with the program participants. I had discovered I had something called empathy. That empathy grew in me with every shift I worked.

How About Now

In 1984, Brenda and I took a trip to Calgary. Brenda has a geology degree too. We met up with some former classmates who'd managed to find work in the field of geology. Only two people from our class got hired into full-time positions. One was a straight-A student with a quadruple major; geology, physics, chemistry, and computer science. Chevron used to send him problems to solve while he was a student. They hired him straight away after graduation.

A few people got hired into term jobs, three or four months at a time. Employers often renewed contracts, but there was no guarantee. My lasting impression was that everybody we talked to was sweating. Competition within their workplaces seemed to heap stress upon them. The threat of layoff hung over their heads every day, and as the economy recovered, laid off experienced geologists would be re-entering the game.

We decided, not yet. We would wait until things got better. Moving to Calgary for a three-month term job just seemed too risky when we both had employment in Brandon. We were both under-employed, but we could pay our rent.

I thought that if I was going to work at B.M.H.C. for a while, I should fully commit to the job for as long as I had it. My curiosity drove me to take every course my employer would approve, and I started to collect a portfolio of certifications, including a series on addictions and counseling. I took several more that led to being seconded to deliver Manitoba Education and Training courses to government employees from all departments. A subtle shift was occurring.

I don't think we ever closed the door to returning to geology; it happened by default. I was learning about myself from my work experience and all the courses. People energized me. I discovered I liked helping people. Now the thought of analyzing drilling core samples in a quiet lab didn't seem so appealing.

THE BRANDON CURLING CLUB

"So you lost. At least you were in the arena of life competing. That's better than those sorry souls who didn't have the courage to at least even try."
Theodore Roosevelt

In the fall of 1984, I formed a new team with Peter, Paul, and Terry. That has a ring to it.

I was new in my job. Peter, Paul, and Terry also had things on the go, so we decided to play only one night a week and enter the Tuesday night men's league. Ed had suggested I go to the Brandon Curling Club because that's where the best teams are. But they weren't playing in the Tuesday night league. I enjoyed the league and looked forward to seeing the guys each week. On the ice, not much was happening. We were making modest improvements as a team. The Tuesday night league, however, was not what we needed to push us higher.

After two years playing Tuesday nights, we decided it was time to move to two nights and play Monday Wednesday, where the big guns were. Paul made the call to enter. They accepted the entry and said we would start in D square. Paul made the point that we'd won more games than anyone else over the last two years on Tuesdays, so we should at least begin in B square.

That fall, we started our two night a week journey in D square. The way it worked was that you played all the teams in your group. If your team had either the first or second-best record after a round, you moved up one square. The two teams with the worst record in the square above moved down.

We decided that we would give the men's zone play-down's a try that year. We called in very close to the entry deadline, before one player told me he had something on and couldn't commit. We scrambled to find somebody. We asked around. Some people we knew declined because they didn't think they were zone play-down material, some had other plans, and all the good ones were already on teams, of course.

We found a guy who accepted, a knee slider. Real good guy – knee slider.

In my first zone play-down as a skip, playing the first stage of play-downs that led to provincials, nationals, and worlds, I had a knee slider playing in the lead position. We lost two straight.

Learning Lessons

We finally landed in A square in the fall of 1986. It was our first look at the best teams in Brandon and their first look at us. Thus began my education in the Brandon Curling Club advanced school of curling. I credit those three years, starting that fall, for teaching me much of what I know about the game. Mostly, it was a school of hard knocks.

These teams exposed flaws in my strategy and weaknesses in our throwing. Everybody played aggressively. There were always lots of rocks in play. It was a hard-knocking school. If I made a mistake and called the wrong shot, the other skip (the teacher) would punish me immediately.

It was a lot of fun. I looked forward to every game. Every night, somebody would teach me a lesson – thank you, teachers. We decided to give zones another go. Our short time in zones the previous year had given us an appetite for it. It would be good to play in an event with something at stake. We still weren't doing any cash bonspieling, but we now knew many of the top local teams.

I didn't see any other zones back then, but I couldn't imagine a tougher one anywhere. Great teams packed the draw, and there were a lot of them. It had to be played over two weekends to get it done. I was pretty excited to get started.

The first weekend went well. We survived the weekend with only one loss. A second loss would have eliminated us. Over half of the field had been knocked out in that first weekend. We got a few slaps on the back and words of encouragement on the way out of the rink.

Curling was all I could think about all week. I was distracted at work. I threw dozens of practice rocks at lunchtime. I couldn't prevent my mind from visualizing shots if I tried. The biggest of the big guns were still there for the second weekend, and I was getting ready.

Our first game of the second weekend was Saturday morning. Brenda was taking her time awakening, this being a day off. She rarely came to watch my games. She had her interests and I, mine, and there were interests that we shared. I popped into the bedroom to kiss her and let her know I was going to the rink.

She sat straight up and looked at me. Her eyes widened slightly. After a brief pause, she said, "Have you got ten minutes? I'm coming with you." She told me later that she saw something in my eyes and wanted to come to the rink to see what this about. I didn't know it consciously but, I was "in the zone."

Team dynamics are a fascinating thing, both when things are going well and more so when they're not. When a skip struggles, a reliable team can keep their focus; keep setting him up until he returns mentally. Confidence can be fleeting, and how a squad deals with a skip experiencing mental vertigo can make a difference.

Likewise, if a skip is on fire, it can be infectious for the rest of the team if they're not there already. We were there and performing at a higher level than we ever had before. One after another, we defeated the biggest names in the zone. We were in the A/B finals. Each team had one loss. The winner would represent Brandon at the Labatt Tankard.

My old Wheat City teammate Dale was playing second on the other team. They were regarded as the best team in southwest Manitoba during this period. We were in tough but weren't lacking in confidence. Our previous wins had us thinking, just maybe, we could pull off another upset.

I was in the zone, in a state of *flow.* The author Mihaly Csikszentmihalyi takes an academic look at flow in his book "Flow: The Psychology of Optimal Experience." I can describe my experience as being in a state of heightened awareness. My senses were acute. I could see and hear everything with sharper contrast. Concentration was focused so that the stimuli that weren't important were blocked out. It was like having a dome or bubble over the sheet, where all you see is the game with increased clarity.

My body was in tune with my mind. I was twenty-five and fit. I'd thrown hundreds of rocks leading up to the competition. My body accepted the direction of my mind.

We played hard, but they were tough and maintained a slight lead through the first half of the game. In the seventh end, we were two down, with nothing going on. The only rock in play belonged to them, a counter in the side of the eight-foot. I decided to freeze. We had to find a way to score a deuce. My weight was perfect, locked on but not shot rock. They decided they couldn't remove it, so they guarded to force me to draw for one. The guard came to rest in a not bad spot. There was no way to tap ours to kick theirs back. They were still shot rock by a sliver, sitting directly behind ours. We decided to go for the sliver. Fearless. We had to throw t-line weight and as it came to a stop, just touch the side of their rock. We made it. Tie game after seven ends.

Of the twenty thousand or so ends that I've played in my lifetime, the next one is the one I've thought about the most. It was the eighth end, tied up, and our opponent had the hammer.

We missed one early, and they got a rock behind a corner guard.

Only an inch of the rock was exposed. I called for a hack weight tap. We could push theirs out of the rings and roll gently to the open, force the play over there and hopefully hold to a blank or one. I knew how to play this like a pro. In "The Curling Book" by Lukowich, Folk, and Gowsell, you learn how to miss on the pro side versus the amateur side. In this situation, missing on the pro side meant that if you didn't get the rock in the house, at least get the guard to clear the path for the next one - don't miss both.

The problem with missing on the pro side is that it's... a miss. I iced it to make it. My third threw it to make it. We flashed past everything as ours grazed past the edge of theirs. They drew a second counter into the open. It came a little deep, to the back of the four-foot circle.

Here's that what-would-you-do thing again. The safe shot was to hit the open one and probably concede a deuce. The high-risk shot was to chase the one behind the corner guard and make the double and get out of the jam. Here are the conditions that led to the decision: it was late - the eighth end, there was no free guard zone rule yet, a deuce was almost certainly a loss. If we gave up a deuce, we'd have to score two in the ninth and steal the tenth. If we only scored one in the ninth, we'd have to steal twice. They had an excellent pealing team. I gave us a five percent chance of winning if they got two in the eighth end. Besides, the way I was feeling that weekend, I could shoot a fly off the top of a match stick. We chose the high-risk shot... and I missed everything.

They drew another rock behind the corner to lay three. Now I had only one shot, to freeze to shot rock at the back of the four foot. I blinked. It felt like the anesthetic wasn't working anymore. The freeze had to be perfect to prevent them from hammering it out. Suddenly, a deuce didn't seem so bad.

I put my broom down, the target for the draw. I had a niggling feeling it wasn't enough ice. The opposing skip had placed his rock there with a slightly in/out release. I knew in my gut that mine would curl more, but I used their broom placement, not mine. I didn't trust my gut feeling. My rock had perfect weight but over curled a few inches. I had shot rock, but they had a tap for a count of four. They made it.

I felt like I woke up during an operation. The sudden turn of events jolted me out of the state of flow. They got one more in the ninth end, and we conceded. There were handshakes and congratulations to the winners. Their third told me to keep my head up and be proud of our run. But my head felt very heavy.

Their team must have been in a state of flow too. They went on to Winnipeg and won the provincial Labatt Tankard, followed by a six and five record at the Brier. We weren't going to stop that train from rolling.

The headline in the Brandon Sun the next morning read "Kujanpaa's Bubble Burst." I'm not sure the writer realized how accurate that was. In the post-game interview, I was asked. "If you could go back and do things differently in the eighth end, would you?" I doubled down and said I would call all the same shots again. In my mind, the only problem was that we didn't make the shots that were called. What would you have done?

Two things happened for me that weekend. One, I got noticed. And two, I discovered that I wanted to live my whole life in a state of flow.

Flow

I had been in a state of flow before. We all have. I'd just never been in as deep as this time.

Curlers have a unique language to describe this

state. The most common description is "in the zone." You'll also hear people say things like "He shot the lights out," "He was feelin it," "She couldn't miss," "She was locked in."

Csikszentmihalyi states. "We have seen how people describe the common characteristics of optimal experience: a sense that one's skills are adequate to cope with the challenges at hand, in a goal-directed, rule-bound action system that provides clear clues as to how well one is performing. Concentration is so intense that there is no attention left over to think about anything irrelevant, or to worry about problems. Self-consciousness disappears, and the sense of time becomes distorted. An activity that produces such experiences is so gratifying that people are willing to do it for its own sake, with little concern for what they will get out of it, even when it is difficult, or dangerous."

Why do I curl? By any objective measure, I should have quit long before I did. The rewards just don't seem to match the effort. There's little money available for a middle-tier competitive player. Big wins are sparse. Fame goes only to the handful of elite players. Why get off the couch on a cold evening in January to drive an hour to Boissevain to play a curling game?

Because this could be one of those nights when everybody's feelin it. You might have a great back and forth game that nobody else cares about in front of an empty lobby. Both teams make one great shot after another, and somebody wins. What a feeling it is to play in a game like that!

You're in a state of flow when you watch TV. You can become so absorbed that you don't notice anything else going on in the house. Two hours seem to pass in an instant. However, passive activities don't offer challenge, complexity, or test skill. For example, you can "zone out" listening intently to your favorite music. On the other hand, if you play an instrument, a jam starting at eight pm can quickly become three am. You won't believe your watch.

When is a person more engaged? Listening to a presentation in a room of twenty people or delivering the presentation in that room?

Curling, like all sports and skill-based activities, is a portal to a state of flow. A key element to achieving this state is finding the right level of competition. Try an experiment. Let's say you're a twenty handicap weekend golfer. Why not challenge the club pro to some straight-up match play. That's likely not fun for either person. Challenge another twenty handicapper to a match and see what happens; it might go back and forth with the outcome in doubt until the last hole. Better still, challenge a fifteen handicapper. He is somebody who presents a more significant challenge, someone less likely to dominate you, someone who might serve to elevate your game.

Imagine a graph where the vertical axis represents the increased skill level of opponents, and the horizontal axis representing your increasing skill level. Where the perpendicular lines intersect is the zone of optimal experience. As your skill level increases, you need more skilled opponents to reach an optimal experience. If your opponent's skill is too far below your own, you will become bored and disinterested. If your opponent's talent is too far beyond yours, you may experience anxiety and mental paralysis.

Years after my high school Rorketon Men's Bonspiel win, I returned. I'd had a taste of higher levels of competition. I played in Rorketon for different reasons now; to support the club, rink burgers, and visit with neighbors. Not so much for the curling itself.

I sat in the lobby, putting on my curling shoes. Another participant was seated across from me, putting on his. He talked about his upcoming game. He was visibly nervous and excited. He hoped he'd win but had his doubts. He was drawn against a good opponent. He went on to say how exciting it would be to win that game because a win would put him in the prizes. He'd never won a prize in the Rorketon Men's before. I thought—*you lucky son of a gun. You've already gotten more out of your game than I will...And we haven't even stepped on the ice yet.*

If we want to watch the Winnipeg Jets play, we know it'll be better to see them against St Louis rather than the Dauphin Kings junior team. But match the Kings with the Portage Terriers and hang on for the ride.

Luckily for me, I've never run short of opponents to

match my skill level. And as good as I got, there were always plenty more that were better than me.

Why did I play? One reason was to chase that feeling of being in the zone. Every achievement sets a new high water mark, and to reach a state of flow; one needs to move up to the next challenge. There's always something a bit bigger just ahead.

We all love an excellent six-five game where both sides have played their best. For some, entering a state of flow happens in the Friday night mixed league. For others, it takes an Olympic final.

If you're an aspiring curler who wants to develop the mental part of your game, there are many good books on the market. One of my favorite curling specific books that includes mental training is "Between The Sheets" by Guy Scholz and Cheryl Bernard.

Super League

In the fall of 1987, I got a phone call. One of the veterans of the Brandon curling scene was putting a team together to play in the Westman Super League of Curling. It was hard to get into the super league. A team was accepted if they'd accumulated enough points in recognized events the year before. The caller and his teammate had points, and I had a few because of my zone final appearance the previous year.

Our total was just enough to get in because our fourth player had none. It was a young guy from Winnipeg, moving to Brandon to take a job. He had also won the World Junior Curling Championships two years before. Bob would be our skip, Jim at third, I would play second, and Larry lead.

Our first game as a team was a battle. Bob made a raise double on two opponent stones in the tenth end to force an extra end. I'd watched him on TV, making that same shot in the world juniors' finals two years before. We'd just won the same way. That was cool.

We finished first in the league. We also played in our only cash-spiel together in Boissevain. I had fun on the ice and off. Many older clubs had a viewing lounge above the lobby, and some had a snake pit below. It was often past the ice-maker's tool room, past the mechanical room, and past the storage room. It was a small room full of cigarette smoke, tin ashtrays nailed to small round tables, and men drinking and telling lies.

It was in there that I found a member of a two time Silver Broom (world) Championship team. He drank and laughed and told stories. I hung on every word. He was a guy I'd watched on CBC Curling Classic while I wore white Bauers, the left one tucked under my right thigh. He indulged a small audience by talking about his famous team's personalities, funny reflections, and a few anecdotes best remaining private.

I watched other curlers kibitz and play mind games with each other and with me. Fun stuff.

In the finals, we played a, then young, Boissevain legend. We prevailed and split a check for twelve hundred dollars.

I sometimes wonder if increasing prize pots resulted in some third-tier competitive players bowing out. In 1987, there was a small circuit of cash-spiels in southwest Manitoba. Entry fees were 160 or 200 per team, and first prize was 1200 or 1600 dollars. At forty or fifty dollars per player, most could afford to gamble on a return. When entries later climbed to a thousand and beyond, it took a suitable bank account, a high level of skill, or sponsorship to play regularly.

Back in the super league, we got a first-round playoff bye for our first-place finish. We won the semi, setting up the final at the Brandon Curling Club. CKLQ radio in Brandon broadcast the game. My parents listened from their home in Rorketon.

Once commonplace, this was near the end of an era for radio broadcast curling.

Here's a sample:

Announcer one: Team 1, throwing yellow rocks, has drawn their stone into the twelve-foot circle, on the tee line. It's the 3 o'clock position in the house.

Announcer two: Yes, it looks like it went deeper than intended. They already have a rock in the eight-foot, in the twelve o'clock position. He has left a pretty easy double.

Announcer one: Team 2, throwing red, is setting up to deliver. The rock is on the way. They yell for sweeping. It looks like he may have turned that one in a bit. They're never off, sweeping all the way...and he makes the hit, but crossed the face by about three inches. His shooter rolls to a stop in the eight-foot at the nine o'clock position. Not what he wanted.

Announcer two: No, he won't be happy with that.

And so it would go.

Unfortunately, that game was a loss for us. It was the last game that the team played together. Bob had committed to playing zones with his team in Winnipeg, and the next year, a career move took him from Brandon.

At the end of season league banquet, Bob was named all-star skip, and I was named all-star second. The players in the league did the voting. In a field that included three provincial championship teams, I was selected at my position. I still feel gratitude to those people for their votes. I had received recognition from my peers.

The next year, I formed a team with Scott, just for the super league. We had two junior age brothers on the front end, Dunc and Doug. I played third. Nobody expected much of us. We were the least accomplished of anybody in the field, and our front end had almost no men's level experience.

A curling reporter from CKLQ reported on the league. Each week, he'd give a preview of the upcoming games, then choose who he thought would win each game. Each week, he would pick us to lose, and each week, we won. Late in the season, we joked with him. "Don't pick us to win now. This is working for us." It was a fun season.

I continued with Peter, Paul, and now Randy in club games and the zones. We lost another zone final that year. It was excruciating because we had an early lead that we couldn't hold.

That spring, I decided to make a big move. I asked one of the most accomplished veteran skips in Brandon to play third with me. He was considered the best player in Brandon not to get to a Brier. I had gained much confidence in my ability to throw skip rocks and reasoned that his presence at third might elevate me further.

I think I was a little surprised when he accepted right away. We were joined by his long time third, who would play second with us. A veteran lead rounded out the squad. I was excited about our prospects for the next season and also nervous about what I'd just bitten off.

Change Is Coming

I was stretched out on the couch on a Sunday afternoon in June. Brenda came in and threw a brand new shirt toward me. She said. "Happy Father's Day," I said. "But I'm not...what...really!" Now I had something way more important to look forward to in the future.

I think I was in a fog for most of the next season. I had a new team, but bigger things were happening. We were going to have a baby, and significant changes were happening with my employer. My job would not exist in its current form next year. We had long conversations about career change options and even moving away from Brandon.

My new team was outstanding, but I struggled to be the team's leader as a skip. I was in over my head. They were very good to me – it was my problem. My last team deferred to me on everything. An opponent's rock would come to rest, and I'd tap the ice where I wanted the broom and take off to the other end to throw. I played quickly. As a skip, there's a rhythm you like to follow.

I became self-conscious. I doubted too many calls. I worried that my highly experienced team disagreed with my strategy. Sometimes, after games, they'd gently offer useful suggestions for what we might have done differently. That only served to erode my confidence. Looking back, we would have been better with the more experienced skip calling and throwing fourth or lining up Ferbey style, with the veteran skipping and me throwing fourth.

We won our share of games despite my challenges. Going into December, we were still one of the favorites to win the Brandon zone. Brenda, now often came to the rink for club games, her tummy growing. She would sit behind the glass and crotchet. Our baby was due in February, the same weekend as the Labatt Tankard provincials. Several of my clubmates assured Brenda that they'd take my place if my team won a provincials berth. Of course, they meant on the ice. Instead, Brenda said. "Great. See you in the delivery room."

My fog didn't lift, and we lost out of zones early. In February, right smack in the middle of Tankard weekend, our daughter was born. She changed our lives for the better and forever that morning.

COMING HOME

"If you can believe it, the mind can achieve it."
Ronnie Lott

Brenda and I spent the summer of 1989 wearing out the walking paths around Brandon. We had a baby coming, and I needed to make a career change. It seemed to us that no decision ever had a one hundred percent clear option. Most seemed to be sixty-forty, and the challenge was to figure out which option was the sixty percent better one. We knew we would miss Brandon if we left.

My dad was turning sixty-five, and mom was about to retire from her teaching position. Something would be needed to be done about the farm. We imagined a quiet farm life, raising kids, 4-H, and fall suppers. We both like the water, and Manipogo Provincial Park (still one of my favorite places in the world) was just nine miles from our farm. We imagined camping with kids, water skiing, and swimming lessons.

In March of 1990, one month after our daughter was born, I took a job at a rehab center in Ste. Rose du Lac. I would commute to shifts to earn income while we got set up at the farm.

Curling has always been part of my life. It's always been there, but it's never been central to my life. I know a few people know me only as a curler, but it's not central to my identity. Curling was something I did in addition to the really important things.

Once I finished the important stuff, the time and energy the game would get depended on whether there was any room left. There had been plenty of room for curling for me in Brandon, but now there wasn't. It was a conscious decision. I wanted to make the other stuff a higher priority. For this, I have no regrets.

I left the hot Brandon curling scene, believing that I might not return to competitive curling – ever. I had lost three win-and-your-in games to get to the Tankard. My attitude was, *oh well, I gave it a shot.*

Goin' To Rehab

There was a lot of work to do to set up our new home. First, I cleared our new yard out of a thick poplar stand with a chain saw. I got help from my youngest brother, who was home from university for the summer, and my dad. We cut and limbed the logs, then piled them for future use as firewood. We removed the stumps with a heavy steel fork mounted on the back of the tractor. I built a lane from the yard to an existing road using hardpan clay topped with gravel. Next, I hired a water well driller to source fresh water for us. Later we'd trench a line directly into the house.

It was exciting to carve a place to live out of a forest. It was also exhausting. I worked on my yard site every spare minute that spring. Haying would start in July and would become our priority. I wanted to get as much set up as I could before then.

I was also in a new job at the rehab center. I came across a worksheet that measured stress. Some of the top stressors were; leaving a job, starting a new career, moving, a spouse leaving a job, having a new child, selling a home, building a house. That didn't include starting to farm. I added up all the numbers attached to those stressors. The key at the end of the document suggested I should be in a state of paralysis. I decided these were all positive stressors, as we'd chosen all of them. We'd get through it.

I entered the field of addictions with some knowledge gained from the courses I'd taken, but there was still much to learn. The support staff position I started in required working both day and night shifts. My curious nature drove me to learn all I could. I wanted to know the answers to some critical questions. How can you definitively diagnose addiction, and what causes it? Where's the line between heavy drinker and alcoholic? What's the prognosis and cure? With my science background, I sought to find clear, concise answers to all these questions and more.

But the science of addiction wasn't as straightforward as geology. Specific combinations of atoms produce particular minerals. The science of addiction seemed to point to things but not with certainty. There must be an answer, I thought. One of the group rooms contained a library cabinet with books by leaders in the field. There were workbooks, pamphlets, and guides from places like Hazelden and the Mayo Clinic. I spent the downtime on my night shifts reading everything in that library. Everything. I watched every video used in the program too. I didn't get the precise answers I was looking for, but I did gain a broad understanding of it all.

I learned the most from the clients themselves. My role was to offer supportive counseling, that is, listening, for the most part. The stories, experiences, and struggles of the people who came to this shelter from the storm gave me an empathetic understanding of addiction to go with the more academic accumulation of knowledge gained from all the books.

Home Town Team

I ran into Russell at a fall supper in September at the Rorketon Parish Hall. The conversation went straight to curling. The Rorketon Curling Club had not previously been affiliated with the Manitoba Curling Association (MCA), meaning a Rorketon team could not enter zone play-downs. Russell had sent affiliation fees in anticipation of my return, signifying a Rorketon team was now eligible to enter play-downs.

That September, a new principal arrived in town for Rorketon School. It was my old friend Stan from university days. Russell suggested Dwayne as a fourth member, and in five minutes, a new team was formed.

I did not anticipate this happening. I knew there were a few good curlers in Rorketon, including Russell and Dwayne. I also knew they were not playing competitively anywhere. When we made plans to move back, I'd entertained the idea of putting a local team together but abandoned the idea. I estimated that there was only a pool of six players at best to make my selection. And none were currently competing.

To be eligible for play-downs, the rules as they were then, said all members of your team needed to be members from the same club. A skip in Winnipeg could select players from anywhere in the city, then buy memberships in the same city club. I chose from a pool of six. The size of your town does matter.

Three of us had cattle, and fall work would slow down a little in November. We decided to go to the "North of 53 berth Bonspiel" in Thompson held in mid-November, and then zones. That would be it. I suggested that maybe we should add a cash-spiel to the schedule as a tune-up.

I entered us in the Keystone Classic at the Brandon Curling Club, the club I missed so much. It wasn't the triumphant return I'd hoped for. We lost three straight. My team's lack of competitive experience was evident. Still, there was cause for optimism. My guys were good curlers. We just had to sort out the weights we threw, communicate, and get on the same page.

The Epiphany

I was working a night shift at the rehab center. Once the busy part of the shift had passed, and the paperwork was done, I headed to the TV lounge for the three am episode of Matlock. I sat there and thought about the competition that would be in Thompson next weekend. I ran the list through my head. I'd heard who was coming from the southwest while in Brandon a week before. There would be others from south-central, a sprinkling of Winnipeg teams, and all the usual northerners.

I thought about what a challenging field it was going to be. I thought about how only one team would win and how many good teams wouldn't. A lot of good teams won't win. But one team will. Then an epiphany. Why not us? Why not us? I repeated the question in my mind and couldn't offer a good reason why it shouldn't be us. I got excited at the thought. I think that at that moment, I gave myself permission to win.

Years later, I heard top-level elite teams talking about "being ready to win." Being ready to win is part physical and mostly mental. The physical part is doing the prerequisite work: practicing proper technique, getting your game in shape to compete.

The mental part is a shift in thinking. Whereas your self-talk may have been "I'm good enough to be in this field," "I can beat anybody here," it goes to "I respect how good everybody is, I'm going to beat them," "I expect to win."

A big part of it is not being afraid to win. What? Winning is great, but there's a part of it that is... well, scary. Going to provincials means being exposed to scrutiny. The lights are brighter, and the competition would be tougher. There would be fans paying to see these games. There would be TV cameras and a press bench with two rows of reporters scribbling notes during your game. When I imagined provincials in my mind, the lights were always very bright. I didn't want to be exposed as a pretender.

Whether a bonspiel in Thompson, a provincial final, or Brier final, a win comes with new implications. You'll invite a wider audience, greater scrutiny, and risk humiliation. I have no personal experience with those higher levels. I rely on the testimony of those who've been there.

Being ready to win means having no fear of what's beyond the horizon. It's to embrace it.

I had decided that we were going to win the Thompson event. I had a six-hour car ride to persuade my team. I felt like I talked the whole time. I don't know if my team thought that I was a little warped or not. We did reach a four-way agreement that we were there to win.

We lost our first game. The grand total of games played as a team was four. We were 0 for 4. We won our next three and qualified for the playoff, but we'd still need three more wins. The verbal agreement in the car was starting to become a belief.

We got early leads in both the quarter-final and semi, then hit relentlessly until the game ended. We'd made the finals. The other team was a good team from Winnipeg.

In the first end, they scored two with the hammer. Disaster struck in the second when the guys from the 'peg stole two to put us down four nothing after two ends. We were still a few years from the introduction of the free guard zone, and I feared they would peel us out.

It seemed like everything I'd ever learned about curling came into play in the next six ends. We manufactured a three-count out of nothing. We stole one. We got in trouble and froze on the shot rock to force a count of one. We battled. A break came in the eighth when they missed twice, and we got some rocks in play. We were one down with the hammer.

When I came to shoot my first, we had a rock top button behind a guard, and the in-turn path blocked. They had second shot stone in the side of the eight behind one of ours in the twelve. The correct shot was to play another on the path to our counter on the button, maybe top eight. But the ice was very straight in that spot, and I worried it would not bury behind the guard, leaving him a double, which would hold us to one.

Everybody in the rink knew the correct shot was the draw just described. His escape hatch, or out-shot, would be to play that path and try to angle freeze my button shot if I left it for him.

I left it for him. I played the short raise onto his rock in the eight-foot to lay four and load the house. We reasoned that it was very straight ice, and he released his out-turn with a slight pop, a small outward motion upon release. We guessed his stone wouldn't curl, and it didn't. His rock came to rest in the top of the four foot, but not buried. It was fully exposed, edge on edge with the guard.

In that spot, hits would back up a few inches, negative ice. We took ice on the inside half of his rock, meaning that my rock would be tracking on the line of the guard upon release. We had to hope it would then "back up" onto the correct line. I chose to throw bumper weight.

The last thing I said to my sweepers was, "Don't jump it." In other words, don't get excited and sweep it too hard too soon. I'd learned a long time ago in Rorketon, sweeping makes a rock back up more on negative ice. If we back it up too much and it hits two thirds, it jams on our rock. We needed to hit it on the nose, with no margin for error.

I released it clean on the path of the guard. My third yelled a quick "Yup." I quickly overruled. "Whoa. Easy." The rock backed up. My third. "Okay, good now" "Just clean."

I watched my rock come within half an inch of the guard and gently tap their rock past ours. We'd scored a five! After a clean ninth end, they conceded. I felt euphoria. I took the steps two at a time, going up to the lounge for the presentation. We were going to the Labatt Tankard. Better yet, Brandon was hosting it in the five thousand seat Keystone Center.

A few months earlier, I had given up on the idea of ever playing in a provincial men's. Now, I was going to play under the bright lights. A place I had subconsciously feared a short time ago.

The Bright Lights

The victory was in just getting there. That's how it is for most first-timers. Your goal is to win a zone or berth bonspiel to get there. When that happens, you realize you haven't spent much time thinking about what you'll do once you get there.

The event itself was everything I'd hoped it would be. The Manitoba provincials have often been described as a mini Brier. It has many of the conditions a Brier has. It has a large paying audience, TV cameras, a press bench. It's always played in arenas that provide a different type of ice than that of curling clubs. And Manitoba had the deepest field in the country.

Three of the top ten world ranked teams resided in Manitoba. There was no guarantee any of them would win because the fourth and fifth-ranked teams were almost as good. Down the line, at least another ten teams had an outside shot at winning the event. In one single game, anything could happen.

It surprised me that the ice wasn't that good. It was

too straight, and the rocks didn't curl much. It was lightning fast, one way. The Keystone Center floor was sloped. When you measure the time it takes a stone to travel from the throwing hogline to the instant it stops, twenty-five seconds is considered good fast ice. The bigger the number, the faster the ice. Rocks timed toward the "uphill" end were twenty-four seconds. Going downhill, we were getting times of twenty-nine and thirty seconds. I had trouble believing my stopwatch.

I remember being vaguely aware of how slow I was sliding and how gently I released the rock. I'd never thrown on ice this fast. Surely, I didn't want my stone to stop halfway down the ice in front of a couple of thousand people. It was unnerving.

I played an aggressive strategy, as usual. This approach has probably been my Achilles heel throughout my curling days. There are times when a bold plan is correct and times when it's better to keep things simple. Strategy 101 would say that one of the times you keep it simple is when you're on new or unknown ice. It's a better strategy to keep it simple until you get a feel for it.

I find keeping it simple, boring. Simple is a winning strategy, but it's more fun to go for it with lots of rocks in play and complicated situations. If I were a hockey player, I'd be the first one into the offensive zone and the last one back to play defense.

Both of our games went down to last rock, with the opposing skips needing to make their shots to claim victory. One of them was the team that eventually won the event. It was an early exit for us but an excellent experience. While we sat in the locker room afterward, the biggest disappointment was not necessarily that we lost, but that losing meant we couldn't play anymore. I wanted to go back onto the arena ice surface and play more. It was definitely going to be an annual goal – to get back to provincials.

If somebody said to me: You only get to play in arenas and play the best teams if you give up the rest, I'd have taken that deal on the spot. It doesn't work that way, of course. To play the bigger events, you have to do the work; practice, travel, seek stronger competition and play. You have to play a lot.

We didn't do the work. I threw a few practice rocks, but we never practiced as a team. With a few exceptions, we didn't travel. Most of the games we played were against teams within an hour's drive. Even at zone play-down time, various team members didn't show up ready to bring their best. One year, I played my first game after coming directly from working a night shift. We all had young families and cattle herds. None of us had more room for curling than we gave it. And it showed.

This period of about six years could have been my curling prime, age thirty to thirty-six. Again, I have no regrets about sliding curling down the priority list. Our son was born in 1993. I remember this period of time being simple, lots of hard work, and family bliss.

We did get back to provincials in 95. Stan had moved on, and Greg replaced him. Lots had changed in the game. Hans, the new provincial ice maker, got more movement in the ice and he sharpened the rocks to react better on arena conditions. It was a thrill to play in the old Winnipeg arena, but we were over-matched. It was another early exit.

RCC

It was great being part of the Rorketon Curling Club again. It didn't have the large membership it once had but was still thriving. Our competitive team split up for league games and local bonspiels. We were all interested in keeping the club healthy. We'd all ask people who otherwise might remain on the sidelines. Over the years, I've tried to make a point of asking neighbors and newcomers to play with me in things like the Farmer's Bonspiel or the Legion, or anything we had going.

Some small communities are blessed with a few natural resources, and Rorketon's best natural resources are its unique and interesting characters. Mike was one of those characters. He was one of the people that curled with me in some of the local events.

He was in his seventies, tallish, slight, and stooped. He wore a tractor hat with the brim locked on at a twenty-degree angle. He had thick black-rimmed glasses, a thin grey mustache, and a home-rolled cigarette that was always stuck to his lip, usually unlit. He spoke with a slow eastern European hillbilly drawl.

He usually had a couple of rye and cokes placed on the window sill while curling. Somebody played a trick and replaced his drink with straight Pepsi. He recoiled like it was poison. People often quoted Mike. He's provided some gems like "I guess the birds weren't singing in our tree today" and "I only sweep the important ones." I was amused that Mike thought mine were the important ones. My uncle was annoyed that his rocks weren't.

I invited a newcomer to town to join our team. Mike had a hard time remembering his name; therefore referred to him as "second man." Four years later, Dave was sure that Mike still didn't know his name, forever "second man."

Mike had his own ideas of how the game should be played. He thought his lead rocks should go in the house no matter what. We were down in a game against an out of town team who was happy to keep hitting with the lead they had. I stood at the hogline and tapped the ice one foot over for a guard. Mike threw his rock right past me and into the house as usual. In the fourth end, I went to him and said. "Give me a guard Mike, and we'll see what happens." He disagreed. I told the sweepers not to sweep his rocks. His usually good draw weight stopped short. We scored two. I said, "That worked good. Can you give me another guard" He did, and we stole a point. We stole every end and won the game. Before leaving the ice, he looked at my third and I. "I don't know how you guys won that game."

He spent the afternoon in the upstairs bar telling everybody exactly how we won the game. He said. "Always listen to your skip." He pointed into the chest of a guy who'd just lost his game. "You know why you lost? Because you don't listen to your skip. Always listen to your skip."

My favorite is a story told by my neighbor Roy. They took Mike to Eddystone to play in their men's bonspiel. Mike embraced the social side of the game and didn't draw a sober breath the whole weekend. At the end of the weekend, sitting in the rink bar upstairs, Mike told Roy he wanted to make a speech. Roy tried to talk him out of it. The room was full of Icelanders with big arms and solo cups full of whiskey. Roy said. "I don't think that's a good idea, Mike."

Mike, "I want to make a speech."

"Mike, the crowd's pretty drunk. It's a bit tense in here."

"I want to make a speech."

Okay. On a Sunday night in Eddystone, in a packed, noisy bar, Roy yells. "Quiet! Quiet, Mike wants to make a speech."

The bar goes quiet, and Mike stands up. "I want to thank everybody. Good bonspiel. Good food. I had a lot of fun. Never been here to Makinak before."

Silence, then a roar of laughter. He had no idea he

was sitting in a curling rink bar in Eddystone.

Mike was a character. I was saddened when I heard he passed. He enriched our lives. Stories about Mike and other Rorketon characters could fill another volume.

A Pause

I looked at my work schedule in the late summer of 1997. I was still working at my temporary off-farm job (it became a twenty-one-year career). We'd joined a Parkland super league the previous two years to get some games as a team. The way my work schedule lined up, I'd have to miss over half the games. I called my team and said I was taking the year off.

There were numerous years when I struggled with how much room there was going to be for curling. The answer probably should have been none at all, at times. We had taken the toe-in-the-water approach. We gave the game little energy but still expected to compete with the teams doing all the work and playing a lot. We were eliminated quickly both times we'd gotten to provincials. There was no reason to believe it would be any different next time.

There were three tiers in competitive curling. Not so much now (more about that later). The first tier includes the elites. These are the household names that play in Briers and tour the country. These players take airplanes to games, not minivans.

The second tier competitive players do some touring too. Most of it is within a reasonable driving distance, one to ten hours. These teams are regulars at provincial competitions. They win some money on the world curling tour and may have a world ranking. Upper second-tier teams can compete with the elites and sometimes move up with the right combination of time, talent, and money.

The third tier is the largest group. These are teams that enter play-downs every year but rarely win. They don't play cash bonspiels unless there's one near where they live. These are competitive people. They'd love to compete at higher levels, but the wrong combination of time, talent, and money prevent it.

We were a third-tier team. I loved to compete and wanted us to be better, but we weren't. We weren't putting effort into it. And so, it wasn't hard to quit, take the year off, and not curl.

The hard part is staying stopped. I started getting itchy around mid-November. I called my friend from Brandon days, Scott. He had stepped back that year too, but we had a plan by the end of the call. He would get a player, and I would find one to make it four. We'd play a cash-spiel in Gimli and then zones. We didn't have much time to pull it together.

The guy Scott found was good. They knew each other within Winnipeg curling circles, and I recruited Brad, originally from Eddystone, now Winnipeg. We positioned Scott's guy at lead, and the Eddystone Eagle at second. Despite having a strong lineup, our first two games were pretty bad. We got thumped handily, and our lead was wanting to move up the lineup. Scott encouraged him to be patient. It might take a few games to find our footing. Our lead went back to Winnipeg and didn't show up for our third game. We played with three players and lost.

Our lead decided that maybe he'd made a hasty decision and called to the rink to see if we were still in the bonspiel. If so, he would come back to Gimli. Scott took his call from the upstairs lounge. He said. "Buddy, we're gone, and you're gone!" Then hung up.

We had a week to find a worthy replacement. I phoned my reliable friend Stan. He had a busy new career, but I argued he should, at a minimum, have enough time to play zones. He got to the rink late for our first game. On the ice, just before the coin toss, I introduced my teammates to each other.

We clicked right away. We played well and won the zone. I had put so much time and effort into curling in my Brandon days and had come up short. This time, we were going to provincials in a year where I'd done next to nothing to earn it.

GOING FOR IT

"This whole journey was never about making a roster or being on a team. It was about giving myself an opportunity. I wanted to take a risk, put myself out there, and put my faith in action. Faith without action is dead. This whole journey, I've never felt so alive."

Jarryd Hayne

The Manitoba Curling Tour was formed in the early nineties. It was created "to provide a means of coordination and support for the series of local bonspiels or cash-spiels in the province."

The MCT turned out to be precisely what tier two competitive teams needed. All the bonspiels were within driving distance, so you didn't need a lot of time off work. Entry fees were lower than on the world tour. It was possible to finance a season yourself or with minimal sponsorship.

The field generally included all the best teams in

Manitoba that weren't the handful of elite teams. The bigger bonspiels on the MCT circuit were also affiliated with the world curling tour. That drew in the elites who liked the option of winning money close to home, money that counted toward the world tour rankings.

Tier two teams want it both ways. They want the lesser disruption to their regular lives that tier three players have, and they want to compete with the big guys. With the MCT, I could feed my cows in the morning, drive a few hours, and play a world champion.

It's part of the beauty of curling's history. The best teams at any moment in history have always been the best teams, but all teams played in the same realm. That's not the case anymore. But in previous decades, a guy like me could kick off my farm boots, put on my curling shoes, and play a famous team; and expect to be able to compete.

Scott and I had enjoyed playing together again. The mini schedule we played the previous year awakened my desire to compete for more. My off-farm work schedule was getting smaller and more manageable. With the support of Brenda and my parents, my kids and cows got fed.

We connected with Peter to skip for us. He is regarded by many as one of the best ever to have a Dauphin Curling Club membership. A young, enthusiastic, hard sweeping rookie would be our lead. We received some generous sponsorship from the Ste Rose Auction Mart. We were well-financed and ready to roll.

We planned a moderate schedule for the fall. Peter and I both had farm obligations in the early fall. The MCT turned out to be a ton of fun. Our new lineup was winning more than losing and earning some prize money. The Curler magazine top ten rankings had us at number eight in the province.

I couldn't wait for zones to come so that we could confirm our spot in the provincials.

The Sickness

I started coughing a week before zones. I spent the weekend resting as much as possible, but I kept coughing. I felt my energy slipping away. On Tuesday, I needed to move some yearlings to another pen. It's a job that requires a little agility and foot speed. My feet felt like they were tied to concrete blocks. Wednesday, I went to the doctor.

He x-rayed my lungs and had me wait. He came in a few minutes later. "You have double pneumonia." Both lungs on the x-ray were black. He said. "We're going to admit you to the hospital."

He went on to say he was prescribing a powerful antibiotic and an inhaler.

It shouldn't matter that the first game of the zone play-downs was less than forty-eight hours away. When you have double pneumonia, that shouldn't be what you're thinking at all. I reasoned with the doctor that staying in the hospital would provide bed rest, and I could just as easily do that at home. He paused and looked me in the eye. "Okay, but go to bed."

I was in Ste. Rose. The lab tech knew me. I heard him say to the doctor. "You're not going to let him go, are you? He's a curler. He's not going to bed." By then, I was halfway out the door.

I got home and phoned Peter. He asked what we should do? The zone chair was a former teammate of Peter's and was not playing in the event. I told Peter that I would see what Friday brings and to ask Ken to bring his shoes.

Then I went to bed. I laid with my upper body propped up to manage the coughing. I chugged Buckley's cough syrup and sweated. I had to change bedclothes regularly after they became drenched.

I got up before six am on Friday morning and had a shower. The sky was still pitch black. I put on my clothes and drove to Minnedosa to play in our first game scheduled for nine am. Go ahead, judge me. It's a teaching moment for your kids. But I'm telling you what happened, not what I should have done.

Minnedosa must have moved its rink since the last time I was there because I had trouble finding it. I walked into the rink just minutes before game time. My team looked at me and asked how I was. I smiled widely and said, "Great! Let's go get 'em." Days later, Scott said it was a fine bit of acting on my part.

Rookie threw the first rock of the game. I leaned in to sweep but couldn't get any pressure on my broom and couldn't get it to move back and forth. I bailed out halfway down the sheet and sat on the bench. I heaved deep breaths. My lungs sounded like velcro being undone.

My turn came to throw my rocks. I made them both. I told the team I was confident I could throw, but it might take a while to get my footing sweeping; besides, the rookie swept hard enough for both of us. After the game, I went to the hotel to lay down and sweat. I did this between every game that weekend. We played three full ten end games on Friday and won them all. I felt marginally better on Saturday morning. I took the fourth of the massive horse pills the doctor had prescribed. My breathing was better, and I swept a few on Saturday. I used my inhaler often.

It's not often you feel better physically going into the seventh game of an event than the first, but I did. The adrenaline was helping. We hadn't lost yet. On that Sunday, we won two more to clinch the zone – undefeated in eight games. We were going to the Safeway Select in Portage La Prairie in February.

Badges

The Manitoba Curling Association (MCA) bonspiel is billed as the biggest competitive bonspiel in the world. In its hundredth anniversary year, there were a record twelve hundred and eighty teams. Every sheet of ice in Winnipeg was needed, and it took a full week to complete.

It attracts the best curlers in the province for two

reasons. The first is that there are berths into the provincial championships available. There are two main events and numerous minor events. If your team reaches the semi-final of either of the main events, you qualify for a provincials spot. Any loss in one of the main event games before Sunday drops you into a minor event (the so-called toaster events).

The second reason is for the momentum the MCA can give a team going into provincials. It's a lot of games, as many as eighteen or twenty. It's played on a variety of ice conditions at various clubs around the city, forcing you to adapt quickly. It gets your game in shape. It can be a grind, but doing well here can set you up for what comes next.

Third-tier teams like it because there's a chance. It's possible you get a soft spot in the draw and don't play anybody too big for a while. You can get on a run, and just maybe, advance to a semi-final and win a spot to the show.

You also get the recreational club curlers. The MCA bonspiel is a unique event. You can enter with your buddies from your Tuesday men's league, get some games, and have some fun.

Our first game was on sheet one at Rossmere, and a recent world champion was playing a weak club team on sheet two. This scenario is one of the reasons rec teams enter the MCA. If you aren't good enough to play for the big prizes, the next best thing is to be drawn against one of the big guys. I love this about the MCA, and curling as it was, in general.

Imagine you're a beer league hockey player and could enter a tournament with the Boston Bruins. It just doesn't happen. But in curling, it did. The club team got walloped. The winning team indulged their request. The amateurs' wives came onto the sheet to take pictures of the teams in front of the lopsided scoreboard. It was a nice moment. I'm sure those pictures still hang in their basement rec rooms.

We couldn't help but notice what was happening on the sheet next to us. Nobody said anything. None of us would be content to be photographed in front of a lopsided scoreboard.

We played the famous team the next afternoon at the Wildwood. They were still one of Canada's hottest teams, just a couple of years removed from their world championship. It seemed they were on TV every weekend, playing in the finals of yet another big cash event. Inexplicably, they had lost their zone play-down in December, probably exhausted from all the games and all the travel.

The MCA was their last chance just to get into provincials. We played them tough. We had a small lead halfway through the game. Cameras from three local TV stations arrived. The newspaper guys were there. I'm sure they had their stories written before they got there. The TV stations would show footage from the game and report how the champ was well on his way to securing his spot in a main event.

But we wouldn't yield. Late in the game, it was evident that an upset was unfolding. We could feel the eyes of players from the other sheets on us. The TV cameras were rolling, getting footage for the supper hour sports news. Our opponents knew it too. Their front end was busy cleaning imaginary debris from the spots where we had just been standing. They gave us "friendly" reminders not to put our knees on the ice. They cleaned imaginary knee spots.

The score was seven to three when they conceded in the ninth end. We won, and the champs lost. Their hopes were barely alive now that they were down to one main event. They couldn't afford another loss.

We watched the throng of reporters and TV cameras stampede right past us to interview the losing skip. The comments he made at that moment dogged him for a couple of years. He stated that the loss was no big deal, really. They didn't place much importance on it. "It's not like we're playing for $20,000 out there. ...We're just playing for badges." The headline in the front of the sports section of the Winnipeg Free Press on January 23, 1999, blared "Choosing Cash Over Glory."

The badges he referred to are the crest you receive when you win a berth into a provincial event. They are coveted by competitive players and admired by club curlers. Most curlers play all their lives and never win a badge/patch/crest.

I do want to cut him some slack. The microphones were in his face before he'd gotten off the ice. In my limited experience with media, I gave at least one horrible interview. A reporter from a local radio station followed me into the locker room and had the tape running before I sat down. I was despondent. Agony dripped off the words in my answers. Later, a couple of people checked in on me to see if I was okay because I sounded so bad. The truth is I was fine five minutes later. There was one quote I'm glad he left out of his report. When asked what was next for our team, I said. "We were going to have a large bonfire and throw all our curling stuff into it." Haha. I was fine. It's just that in the moment, it's hard to see a healthy perspective. A short time later, you can.

It must have stung to lose to us. They were on top of the world. How do you explain what happened? One way is to diminish the importance of the game. It's hard to explain losing to a lesser opponent in a game that matters. If the game doesn't matter - no big deal. And so I think the money over badges comment was an attempt to wave off the outcome. There were bigger fish to fry. He had a point. It actually cost money for people to play in a Brier. That changed soon after as a result of a boycott of the Brier by the top WCT teams. The "Original 18" best teams in Canada boycotted the Brier for two seasons beginning in the fall of 2000.

From their perspective, cash ruled over badges. Rank and file curlers didn't see it that way. The comment set off a firestorm of controversy. Many curlers felt they had disrespected us and, by extension, had disrespected all of them. He had trashed the badge, the crest that so many players had come to value.

We became folk heroes to the common curler. For the rest of the week, everywhere we went, every club we walked into, people wanted to talk about it. Some thought it was pretty dismissive of him. We weren't a team of nobodies; we were ranked eighth in the province and previewed to be contenders in the upcoming provincials. Others saw themselves in us. We were the ordinary guys that beat the pros. We were the kind of team that could keep the dream alive for all curlers. If it could happen for us, it could work for them too. We were not that unlike they were. We represented the Everyman team.

Don't count the champs out. They went on a run in the other major event in the bonspiel and got their meaningless patch and a berth into provincials. We also had a good run. We managed an eleven and zero run before our first loss. Combined with the games from our zone, our winning streak was 19 and 0.

At the Safeway Select in Portage La Prairie, at the opening banquet, the guest speaker gave an impassioned speech. He reminded curlers not to lose sight of their roots; no matter how big you get, don't forget all the other important people in and around the game. Remember your parents for driving you to the rink. Remember the ice makers, the coaches, and endless numbers of volunteers who did things because they love the game – not for the money.

The second from the team of villains sat back in his seat and waved a couple of twenty dollars bills. The controversy didn't need to go on as long as it did, but it seems twenty dollar bills are good for fanning the flames.

The Big O

We sat in a hotel room with some other players who were eliminated from the competition. It had been an interesting year. We told our stories, and they told theirs.

The door was open to the hallway. Into the room walked the 1972 Silver Broom Champion, the Big O. I was eleven years old when I watched Boots LaBonte, of the United States, jump into the air to celebrate his apparent win. He slipped, fell, and nudged the Canadian stone far enough to count. A measurement confirmed it and the game was tied. The Canadians played a near perfect extra end to steal the World Championship from the Americans. Legend has it that it was the curse of Boots LaBonte that prevented gold for Canada until 1980.

The Big O had a couple of paper bags in one hand and a bottle of whiskey in the other. He asked if anybody would like to join him downing a clove of garlic, then eating a chunk of kulbasa, and chasing it with whiskey.

This guy was the Big O. If curling were a religion, this is like the Pope asking you if you want to do communion. Of course, I said yes.

The Big O went on to tell a story that should never

appear in print. There was another round of garlic/meat/whiskey. And then he left.

Peter and I went back to the arena the next morning. We thought we'd catch a game before making the trip home. We overheard a couple of people sitting behind us: "Do you smell garlic?"

We both smiled but dared not look at each other.

Sometimes late at night, if the stars are out, and if the campfire is still crackling, and you pass me a guitar, I might sing this song. It's called The Stories We Could Tell. Tom Petty wrote the original; it was about touring musicians. I changed the verses to be about curlers.

The Stories We Could Tell   Key of D

Talkin to myself again, wonderin if all this travellin is good
If there's somethin better doin, we'd be doin if we could

And oh the stories we could tell
And if this all blows up and goes to hell
I can still see us sittin on the bed of some motel
And listenin to the stories we could tell

Remember that big shot we had
The score was tied and the ladies got so mad

And the aches in our knees tell of all the games we played
And all of the stories we could tell

And oh the stories we could tell
And if this all blows up and goes to hell
I can still see us sittin on the bed of some motel
And listenin to the stories we could tell.

So if you are a curler and freezin every night
And your playin for a sponsor neath the frosty colored lights
And if you ever wonder why you ride this carousel
You did it for the stories you could tell

And oh the stories we could tell
And if this all blows and goes to hell
I can still see us sittin on the bed in some motel
And listenin to the stories we could tell

The opening chapter describes the last shot of the WCT final in Dauphin. There's a bit more to it. The local radio station CKDM was doing remote updates from the rink all day. More people came to the rink after our quarter-final win, then the semi, and even more filed in to watch the final. By the time we got to the last end, it was a huge crowd.

It felt good. I thought - this is Dauphin, and I'm playing a team from Saskatchewan. Everybody's with me.

I had a vague sense that a big part of the crowd were women. I didn't think anything of it. After we made the last shot, women poured out onto the ice. I'd lost track of the fact that we were playing the final on a Monday, and Monday is Women's League night.

The bonspiel organizers had persuaded them to remain in the lobby until our game was over. It turns out, many of them were annoyed with us. WCT, never mind, it was their league night.

The line in the song "remember that big shot we had, the score was tied and the ladies got so mad" refers to that moment.

Why do I curl? Sometimes it's just for the stories I could tell.

CATTLE

"You look at a herd of cattle and well, they all look the same... but they know.
They all have an individual personality, and those personalities change from day to day. They can have their grumpy days and their happy days and their serene days. But it's unpredictable. You can't be off in outer space when you're dealing with animals."

Chris Cooper

Cattle ranching is hard work. It can be hard to understand the attraction. Cattle ranching appeals to the fierce independence in a person. You have no boss and nobody to answer to. You wake up early in the morning and work long hours because it's yours. There's no shift coming in to clean up your laziness. A ranch is like a portrait you've painted – one that you keep coming back to, to touch up. You repair a fence and re-seed an old field to alfalfa. There's work waiting for us every day.

Ranching is, for the most part, a romantic notion and a harsh reality. At its best, there's nothing more rewarding. I enjoyed going to the pasture in early June to check the herd. They were off of winter feed and out on the range on their own. Short, shiny, healthy hair replaced their shaggy winter coats. They stand together in bunches, lush grass up to their knees. Others lay content in shady poplar and willow bushes. In the late afternoon, they parade to the water hole for a long drink.

Haying season begins in late June and lasts two and a half months if the weather cooperates. It's a time when there's work that can be done all day, every day, and it's summer. I had to find ways to take time to relax. Brenda took the kids for two weeks of camping at Manipogo Beach for swimming lessons every year. It was only nine miles from our farm. I drove out to meet them for supper as many times as I could. We'd swim, roast marshmallows, and water ski if the lake looked calm. I bought an old ski boat when we moved to the farm. For eighteen hundred dollars, I got a boat, motor, and trailer. I left it at the park so that we could launch it quickly anytime we had the chance. It got well used.

Haying equipment had changed from the time I was a kid. Now, we gathered our hay into fifteen hundred pound bales instead of haystacks. Our best tractor had a cab with a radio and air conditioning. One at a time, our kids would sometimes join me to get some extra time with me and be part of the operation. Our daughter learned to cut hay and to make a bale. It became a routine task very quickly. The two of us spent most of our time together talking about whatever came to mind: the kids at school, the Meech Lake Accord, the Cuban missile crisis. I'm not sure how we got on to this range of topics. CBC radio, which was on in the background all the time, likely cued our subjects for discussion. She was born with some of my curiosity.

Our son is a few years younger and was more about the farming. World events were much less important than getting the field finished before the rain. He sat on the edge of the seat, barely able to see over the dash. He stretched his left foot forward as far as he could to depress the clutch. He knew the routine; bale indicator light turns solid green, he pushes the clutch to stop the tractor, and shifts into reverse and back up fifteen feet. When the bale is tied, the green light flashes; disengage power take-off, pull right side hydraulic lever back to open baler hatch. Drive forward, fifteen feet. Push the hydraulic lever forward to close the baler hatch. Re-engage power take-off, and proceed into the windrow until you have another full-sized bale.

Dale, with great detail, described this process to his mother. Brenda listened intently and concluded. "Wow. That's pretty good. I think that if you know how to make a bale, you can probably operate a washing machine." Our kids washed their clothes and made their own school lunches from a young age. In fall and winter, they worked together on their after school chore. Their job was to fill one hundred and eighty feet of troughs with barley for the cow herd. They filled the troughs carrying the barley in five-gallon pails. It needed to be done every second day. The most challenging days were when we got a heavy snowfall, and they had to clean the snow out before loading the troughs with barley.

The two busiest seasons for me were haying and calving time. Calving started in mid-February. The majority of calves were born in the first forty-five days, but there were always stragglers into April. In February, when it was cold, the cattle had to be checked at least ten times a day, round the clock. I did the night checks. I'd set the alarm, get dressed, and jump on the Ski-Doo to ride over to the calving grounds. It was a two-acre area that contained the whole herd for calving time only.

Cows

Sometimes, I'd take a moment to stop and look at the sky and watch the billions of stars or a good show of northern lights. There was no light pollution out there, and it was often a brilliant display. I'd walk through the herd quietly with a cane. I always had something in my hand in case I had to persuade an overprotective new mother not to trample me. Usually, I just used it to scratch their backs as I walked past them.

The cattle knew me as one of them. They wouldn't get up if they were already bedded down for the night.

They knew my walk, the smell of my barn clothes, the sound of my voice if I said something to them in a low tone. "Hey girl. Looks like you're getting close. When you gonna have your calf?"

A friend asked if he could come with me one evening. He was curious to see what checking cattle was all about. I lent him some of my spare work clothes. It didn't fool the cows. They watched us, specifically him, as we meandered through the nervous-looking herd. I'd advised him not to speak while we were among the cattle. They wouldn't recognize his voice and would be suspicious. Afterward, I asked him about his experience. He said, "I felt like I was walking through a biker bar in a leisure suit."

I was checking so regularly because, of course, calves are born wet. If they're born outdoors in subzero temperatures, they can suffer damage to their ears and feet especially. We had a large shelter bedded with fresh straw every day. If they calved in there, they'd be okay with all the body heat from other cows. But all too often, a cow would go off by herself to have her calf. So, at three in the morning, I'd enter the calving yard and scan the perimeter fence with my flashlight. Sure enough, I'd see a cow's shiny eyes looking back at me.

If she hadn't calved yet, I'd coax her into the maternity barn. We used the Temple Grandin philosophy of low-stress cattle handling. I'd approach slowly, slightly behind and to the side of her hip until she felt just uncomfortable enough to start moving. I'd guide her to the barn by moving in and out of her flight zone and moving up to her front shoulder if I wanted her to stop. Minutes later, she'd be in the maternity pen without knowing how she got there.

If she calved before I got out for my check, I'd get the calf sled and roll the wet calf onto it. This is the time when a cow is most dangerous, immediately after calving. I had a thirty-foot rope on the sled to pull it. That way, the cow could continue to lick her calf and follow the sled as I brought them both toward warmth.

Bull

Bulls, on the other hand, can never be trusted. Frequent exposure to machinery and livestock makes ranching one of the most dangerous occupations in Canada. I had a Texas Longhorn cross bull that I used on first-calf heifers. The large-boned exotic cows we had produced lots of beef, but they were also prone to birthing complications. Longhorns are known for hardiness and having low birthweight vigorous calves, a result of natural selection after decades as a feral breed in south Texas.

My longhorn developed a case of foot rot, an infection in the hoof and ankle area. The treatment is an antibiotic. I walked up to him and using a spring-loaded syringe on the end of a harpoon-like stick; I gave him his first treatment. He didn't like it, and I had to give him a second dose the next day. He tried to avoid me by going into a mud hole, hoping I wouldn't follow. I had to be careful. If my boots got stuck, he'd surely maul me. I managed to get a second dose into him, which really pissed him off.

His foot healed, but he went wild, retreating to his more feral instincts. I couldn't even enter the pen he was in after that. If he heard the latch, he'd start pawing and snorting. He would have to be shipped to market. It was too dangerous to keep him on the farm any longer. But I couldn't chase him into the stock trailer. If I tried, he'd turn to charge me, and I'd have to hop a fence. I needed to move him through three pens, then a sorting area before getting him into a narrow alley leading to the trailer.

I couldn't chase him. I'd have to let him chase me. I opened all the gates to the pens leading to the trailer. Then I opened the entrance to his area last, swung it wide open, and stood there. He charged, I ran. I ran alongside the fence. If he got too close, my escape was to hop the rail fence. The plan worked. I ran through one pen after another with that crazed longhorn on my heels. I jumped the rail fence in the alley to the trailer, doubled back, and slammed a gate behind him. With nowhere to go, he quietly stepped into the trailer, and I closed the door behind him. I made sure to inform the auction staff to be extra careful with this one.

Three Bulls

I got a call from a neighbor one hot July evening

because his three bulls had broken a fence and entered my pasture and my herd. We made a plan to retrieve them the next day. My summer pasture was an isolated expanse, sixteen hundred acres of bush, native prairie grass, and swamp. I would enter the range from the east on an ATV and try to find them. My neighbor would bring his tractor and stock trailer down an abandoned pioneer road allowance. He used his chain saw to cut his way in where the trail narrowed too much.

I found one of the bulls among my cattle, sitting in the shade of a poplar bush on the edge of an old field. Perfect, we could get the trailer to that clearing. I had three bags of grain with me. I opened one and poured it into small piles on the ground at the edge of the field. Anytime I pasture checked cattle, I brought a treat. When they heard me coax them, "c'mon," they got up and began eating from the piles.

The bull got up and helped himself too. While he was busy munching, I got my tranquilizer syringe ready. A two cc dose was enough to make a two thousand pound bull very sleepy. If I accidentally got myself, lights out. I carefully placed the syringe into the spring-loaded harpoon, walked behind him, and gave him a shot in the ass. He didn't even look up, content to finish his treat.

I waited for the tranquilizer to take effect and waved at my neighbor to bring his trailer over. The bull walked a few steps, then decided he should sit down. He started snoring with his eyes open. We had to act fast and get him loaded before he got too relaxed. If he slowed down too much, we'd have to wait hours for the effects to wear off enough for him to stand up again.

We quietly carried fourteen-foot steel panels and built a small pen around him. Then we backed the stock trailer up to one side and prodded him to stand up. He stepped right into the trailer. That was easy, one down.

We used the same process when I found the second bull. This time, when we secured the steel panels around him, the sound of the latch pin dropping into place startled him. He got up and ran a hundred yards pushing the steel panel pen with him. Eventually, he got tired, and we loaded him too.

The third bull was a massive black Angus with a suspicious nature. I got a shot into him without any trouble and waited for him to snooze. It started to rain. The sight of the three of us hauling fourteen-foot steel panels through a thundering downpour was surreal. We got to the bull and tried to put the steel panels around him as quietly as possible. He was still on alert and got up and ran to the edge of the bush. We couldn't let him get in the bush. We wouldn't be able to get a trailer in there.

The revised plan was for me to sneak around him through the bush and give him another two cc's of tranquilizer from behind. His escape route from me would be back to the field. It worked, and soon he stretched out on the grass again. We decided we'd try to get a lasso on him. That way, if he got scared when we backed up the trailer, we could quickly wrap the other end of the rope on a bumper and prevent his escape. I approached slowly, and he got up again a ran a short distance, but I'd gotten the lasso on him.

We gave him time to settle down. My neighbors and I took a moment to have some water and energy bars. We were soaked and filthy. I looked down at my t-shirt and jeans. The dust was now mud, and the rusty residue from the steel panels ran in red streaks across my chest. It was getting late, and the bull, despite a double dose of tranquilizer, was on high alert. He wasn't settled. I gave him one more dose to counteract all the adrenaline flowing through him. We backed the trailer toward him quickly and wrapped the rope around the bumper.

    He lurched back to escape and almost choked himself to death. We released the pressure in time and coaxed him from behind to step toward the trailer. With each step, we pulled up the slack in the rope. We fed the rope into the trailer and wrapped it around a steel support structure. The bull pulled back and bent it, so we had to re-release a bit. It was like trying to reel in a twenty-two hundred-pound fish that wants to kill you.

We got him and trailered all three of them home. It took us all day. My neighbor said the Angus slept for three days. These were some of the things I did in curling's offseason.

KEEP IT SIMPLE

"Moment of victory is much too short
to live for that and nothing else."
Martina Navratilova

I was back to skipping in the fall of 2000. I'd put together a team of keeners. We had sponsorship and planned to do a few more MCT and WCT events. I liked the enthusiasm we had on the team. My new teammates had never won anything of note but wanted to move up the competitive food chain.

And they were willing to do some work to get there.

We had success right away. We won some money, qualified for the MCT championships, and won a berth into the Safeway Select. This year was the honeymoon stage of team development. When you first put a team together, everybody is playing to impress his teammates and "make the team." Comments are positive and encouraging, and there is hope for what is possible for the team.

Over the course of a few years, this team performed exceptionally well. But with some success, increased expectations can arise. We decided to go pro, meaning that we should adopt some pro habits ourselves if we wanted to compete with the pro teams.

We threw scores of practice rocks individually and had team practices. We improved but tried not to be complacent. We were qualifying in cash bonspiels regularly and had shown up on the WCT rankings. By that measure, of all the teams in the world, we had crept into the top one percent.

A cash bonspiel is a stand-alone event. Thirty-two teams enter. Eight will qualify for the money, and only one team will win first prize. That means that for thirty-one teams, the last game was a loss. The lasting taste in your mouth would be a loss, even if you finished ahead of most of the field.

We won five thousand dollars for making the semis in Swan River one year. Yet all we could talk about was a miscommunication in the semi-final game that led to the loss. We never wanted to be satisfied with where we were because that would drive us to be better. That meant we were never satisfied.

Let's say every team in the field was of an equal caliber, for the purpose of discussion. We could say, in that scenario, that we could beat anybody in the bonspiel. It would be equally valid that anybody could beat us. Finishing last would be just as likely as finishing first. All things being equal, the deciding factor would come down to intangibles, performance, and execution. That part of the game exists between the ears, for the most part.

None of us were pros, so we guessed at what that meant. We got some of it right and some of it not. We collaborated on a written game plan. There was a plan for each end of the game, each scenario. After games, there were times a player questioned our approach. That was good. We had followed the game plan. Did we want to revise it? Often we concluded that the missteps were problems with performance or execution rather than the strategy itself. Having a game plan is a good thing, in my opinion.

We got tangled up with our notion of systems; the weight we threw for hits, the timing of rocks, split times. The four of us had different sliding speeds meaning the split number was different for the same shot. Front end: "I don't know why it was light. You nailed the split." The numbers didn't matter. The rock was thrown too light. We had over-complicated our execution. We needed fewer numbers going through our heads, not more.

Training

I learned more about high-performance training a few years later, when my son played in the Manitoba games. I coached the team. They were invited to a high-performance curling camp (along with all the other Mb. Games teams) at the Granite in Winnipeg. The Manitoba representative to the Canada games would be selected from this group.

They had on and off-ice training sessions. There was an in-depth delivery analysis. There was a "speed trap" to teach the use of stopwatches on split times. They used a laser to teach sliding direction and the Dartfish program to do an in-depth computer analysis of the delivery. Off the ice, they had strategy sessions with a world champion and worked on development plans.

I couldn't help but picture myself walking down Portage Avenue, with my hand-sewn shoe bag over my shoulder, all those years ago.

Lofty Goals

Despite our relative success on the MCT, our real goal was to do some damage at provincials. We imagined ourselves competing with the provinces best. We convinced ourselves we deserved it because we were working so hard and wanted it so badly.

A little self-delusion can help a curler. You truly need to believe you're better than you are, just to be in the game. Without delusion, your belief may waver, and you stop playing like you expect to win. I've never met a competitive curler who wasn't at least a little deluded.

We deluded ourselves into believing we could win a provincial title. Four teams from western Manitoba had done just that in my time. These were peers, people we often played against, people we sometimes beat. We could compete with them, and if we could compete with them, we could achieve what they had achieved.

We entered zone play-downs with high expectations and high anxiety. In my estimation, the curling gods often do course corrections for you; and they saw fit to have us lose the zone final on the last rock. We had lofty goals and couldn't get out of the zone. The loss dealt us a heavy dose of humility.

The second stage of team development is storming. In the storming stage, there is conflict, resistance, and high emotion. We experienced all of it. Most teams don't survive this stage. The very best teams do. The next step is norming, a reconciliation stage that lowers anxiety and builds cohesion. The third stage is followed by performing, where a healthy team is capable of anything.

I watch high-level teams with admiration. I see them suffer severe losses, only to return and challenge again. I've rarely been on a team that got past storming. Most of my teams were barely into the forming/ honeymoon stage when changes came.

This experience was another of the great lessons gleaned from the sport. Our team was made up of four good people, friends with a common goal, and somehow we imploded under the weight of expectation. Mihaly Csikszentmihalyi states: "The challenges of competition can be stimulating and enjoyable. But when beating an opponent takes precedence in the mind over performing as well as possible, enjoyment tends to disappear. Competition is enjoyable only when it is a means to perfect one's skills; when it becomes an end in itself, it ceases to be fun."

We'd lost sight of the shot right in front of us because our attention was on something further in the future.

Our team also had a perfectionist personality on it. In the book "Sports Psyching" by Tutko and Tosi, the perfectionist is described: "He tends to become impatient with himself, to demand too much, to measure himself against too high a standard, to ignore improvements and dwell on his shortcomings instead of evaluating the game in its own context."

"Much of what the perfectionist does is self-defeating. He wants to improve performance, but ironically, by setting overly ambitious goals, he sets himself up for constant anxiety. The tensions thus created interfere with the very performance he wants to perfect."

Why do we play? Is it for the prize? A plaque? Or some trophy? Is it for the money that gets spent on the entry into the next cash bonspiel? Is it for the respect of your peers? Maybe for some kind of external validation that comes from the praise and accolades afforded by others? Do we play for fame or a place, written in ink, in a history book? And is it enough to justify the effort?

I often think of sports as a metaphor for life. We might be part of a team at work, where the challenges are significant, and unforeseen circumstances challenge the team's strength and cohesion. It's what we learn about ourselves when challenged that is most valuable. It's easy to be a team player when things are going well. How good are you, collectively, when things aren't going well? I sometimes said after losing a curling game: "I wonder what that was about. I already have enough character."

Every year, only a few teams make it to the Brier. Only one team wins the world championship. Why do the rest of us curl? What's in it for us, you and me? These were the questions I was contemplating in the spring of 2003.

BSE

I heard the news while having lunch at the Chicken Chef in Ste. Rose in May of 2003. People at the next table told me a cow in Alberta was discovered to have BSE, mad cow disease. I lost one hundred thousand dollars of equity in my herd that day.

WHAT NOW

"If it's not fun, tell me, why are you still playing?"
unknown

It's hard to give up on a dream. In 2003, I gave up on two of them. I wanted to be a championship curler, and I wanted to be a cowboy. I didn't have to give up on either one of those dreams. Nobody made me give up. I was the one who chose to turn my back.

We often hear: "Persevere...never give up." Yet, it is when I quit that I experienced some unexpected rewards behind another door.

When I gave up on cattle ranching, I entered the most rewarding and satisfying phase of my working life. I re-dedicated myself to my "off-farm" job, which was my career all along. I threw myself back into the learning and personal growth that is an inevitable part of that field. I was an addictions counselor specializing in process addictions, specifically gambling.

New Perspective

But I didn't give curling up entirely. I just stopped swimming upstream. The previous season had felt like I was white water rafting, paddling furiously upstream to see what was around the bend, just beyond my reach. When you turn the raft around and go with the current, hang on, it's going to be a fun ride. Paradoxically, the more I let go of the desired outcomes, the better the results became. I focused more on the process, the execution of a good game plan, one shot at a time. It would be fun again.

I would also be back to a smaller bonspiel schedule. It's not easy to get out of cattle ranching quickly. It would take three years to phase out, to manage the debt and tax liabilities. It wasn't until December of 2006 that the last smelly arse ran up the ramp and into the truck.

Kids

This stretch was a busy time for our family. Both our daughter and son were multi-sport high school athletes. I coached each of them at curling provincials, but both excelled most at volleyball. Both were selected as provincial all-stars among single and double-A schools in Manitoba. We shared in the joy of competing. We spent time around the dinner table, discussing ways to overcome the unwanted circumstances that sometimes interfered with our desires, including challenging team dynamics. Often the conversation was just about how great it was to compete.

I was hopeful that our kids could apply the lessons learned from sports to other areas of life. I think they got it. Healthy active living is a part of their lifestyles, and I think they are great teammates among their peers in their schools, workplaces, and communities.

The Bar Shift

I continued to compete through this period too. If being healthy means nurturing body, mind, and spirit, curling was one thing that ticked all three boxes for me. These years were a time where I was back to giving curling a little less room. I didn't want to miss volleyball tournaments.

I rediscovered the joy of playing in our small town bonspiels and all that went with that. When you live in a small town, everybody knows your business. That's both good and bad. There are plenty of stories of how the community pitches in if something unfortunate happens. Suppose a family's home burns, the community rallies to provide necessities. If a farmer is injured, neighbors will come and do the chores. People care for each other.

One day, sad news circulated through the rink. A local farmer had died. People were surprised and saddened. And then, the supposedly dead farmer walked through the front door of the curling rink. Somebody yelled, "Hey, I heard you were dead!" The farmer wore a big goofy grin on his face and replied, "No, not yet. I gotta work my bar shift." He hadn't heard the news.

My Neighborhood Team

I usually called around my neighborhood to scare up teammates for local bonspiels. My local community was the six households within a thirty square mile quadrant north and west of my house. One of my regulars was a single guy from a few miles down the road. He leads an uncomplicated life, rarely coming to town except for groceries or farm supplies. Part of the fun for him was all the stuff you could get at the rink; burgers, treats, all the bar and concession junk. When we played, he left the ice frequently to buy treats, use the washroom, and who knows what. One particular game came down to the last shot. I needed to draw to the four foot to win. As I settled into the hack, I saw one sweeper but not my neighbor. I could see past the end of our sheet of ice and through the glass into the lobby. He was at the concession buying something. I could see his head swivel back and forth. He could see I was getting ready to throw, and his coffee was being poured. Should he stay or should he go?

I smiled and threw my rock. My one sweeper did all she could, but the rock came up a few inches short. My neighbor came crashing out onto the ice with coffee running down the back of his hand. He'd gotten there just in time for the post-game handshake. Thanks for the game.

Draw Weight

A character from my school days, decades earlier, resurfaced. I asked him to play a few games. We played a club game on a chilly night in February. He played lead and threw his first rock right through the house. Then he threw his second rock through the house. Good curlers are usually able to make the adjustment after one shot and find the right weight after that. This guy hadn't played for a while, so I thought it might take a bit longer. In the second and third ends, he fired his rocks through the house just as hard. In the fourth end, after firing his seventh consecutive rock through the house, he slid up to me and asked, "Do you want me to throw those a little lighter?" He wore an entirely earnest expression on his face. I answered just as thoughtfully, "Sure. That way, they'll stop in the circles." He nodded and slid away.

Animal

Occasionally, I ventured out to the neighboring communities to participate in their local bonspiels. I went to Eddystone and found myself in a good battle with the best hometown team. The second on the team was nicknamed "Animal" due to his uncanny resemblance to the Muppet drummer and his general approach to life.

Animal swept hard until his skip's rock came to rest. It was a particularly good shot. Animal's momentum had him slide right past where I was standing, at the back of the house. As he skidded by, he said, "Put that in your pipe and smoke it!" Beautiful. That was why I came to Eddystone.

The Reunion

Thirty years after my high school team won the Rorketon Men's Bonspiel, we decided to reunite. Two of the guys now lived in Winnipeg, one was in The Pas, and I was back in Rorketon. It was great getting together again. So much had happened since high school. We all had lots to tell each other. We laughed at the stories from back then and re-lived past glories. At least a few Rorketon people thought it was amusing that the current version of "the kids" had gotten together once more. Many remembered that bonspiel all those years ago. The older versions of ourselves were all still curling, and we won again. It wasn't as exciting as the first one, but the time with old friends was priceless.

I dipped my toe back in on the competitive side too. I jumped into the lineup of a Winnipeg based team to play a memorable MCA bonspiel.

I played a couple of shortened seasons with the Swan River boys. Our third had recently played in a Brier, but our front end had almost no competitive experience. That didn't matter because they weren't intimidated by anybody. They were curlers. We had a zone win and a good time at provincials.

I played third with the Virden guys for another

short season. That year's highlight was a trip out west and a game against the legendary 1976 and 1978 world junior winner. I was just coming out of the shadows of cattle ranching. Things were about to get a bit easier. The cattle were gone, my land was rented, and I would have a decent amount of holiday time again.

Back In Gear

In 2008, I formed a team with Woody. Sean brought competitive pedigree at second, and we recruited a rookie, Justin, at lead. We got together with our families at Falcon Lake one weekend. It was a chance to get to know one another better and plan our winter schedule. We knew each other as competitors. There was mutual respect. But you always see the better side of people as teammates, in my estimation. Our team clicked.

That winter turned into a very enjoyable season for me. We won our share of games on the cash circuit; we won our zone and had a promising start to the provincials before being eliminated. And we got on a great run at the MCA.

Back in the Parkland area, I joined another team for super league curling only. My teammates had long-distance competitive teams too and wanted to play in something else locally. That worked for all of us, and we won the league championship.

I caught the fever again, and life circumstances were going to allow a busier schedule next year. Our team committed to each other for another year.

The Dog

I did wonder if other psychological factors were at work when it came to my continued play. I actively contemplated quitting competitive curling many times, but it was always temporary. Throughout my career, I was painfully aware of the behavioral concept of intermittent reinforcement. Intermittent reinforcement is a conditioning schedule in which a reward or punishment is not administered every time the desired response is performed. For example, if you want to teach your dog a trick, give him a dog treat every time he performs the trick (continuous reinforcement). Another approach is not to give a treat every time; make it every few times. It's better if the rewards are random and unpredictable. Just for kicks, give him a hamburger once in a while, and occasionally a steak. This type of conditioning increases the likelihood the behavior will last longer. In the dog's subconscious mind, he gets a steak every time he does the trick correctly. It's what makes gambling so addictive.

This kind of conditioning schedule can cause a positive, even euphoric response in the brain. I couldn't help but think of how the rewards arrived for me in curling: win – treat, loss - no treat, a run of wins - hamburger, win an event – steak. I wouldn't enter a competitive event if I didn't think the figurative steak was possible every time.

UNDER THE KNIFE

"We love to expect, and when expectation is either disappointed or gratified, we want to be again expecting."

Samuel Jackson

I couldn't wait for the 2009 season to begin. We planned to do a slightly larger schedule, thanks to an abundant amount of holiday time again. With an excellent first season together behind us, we felt there were bigger things in store.

The first bonspiel on our schedule was in late September. I was in Winnipeg a couple of weeks earlier to attend my son's volleyball tournament. West Kildonan already had ice in, so I booked some practice time.

I found that the older I got, the more I needed to pay attention to my body, particularly my knees and legs. My pre-game routine now required a minimum of thirty minutes of stretching, starting at home or the hotel room and finishing at the rink. I rushed from the volleyball game and did some stretches at the rink, but not enough.

These were going to be the first rocks of the year, and I hadn't spent much time preparing my leg muscles for that unique tuck position, reserved only for delivering curling rocks. I only had an hour of ice time booked and didn't want to waste it stretching. I did a practice slide that felt stiff. My left heel didn't come anywhere near the correct notch on my right thigh. I slid several more times.

In the past, if my legs weren't warmed up all the way, a few practice slides seemed to remind my muscles of their duty. It wasn't happening this time. I threw a few rocks, thinking that would do the trick. It didn't. Instead, the left knee got tighter.

I decided to keep throwing. There wasn't any ice ready back home. This moment was my only chance to throw practice rocks before our first bonspiel. It was the wrong decision.

I undressed in the locker room and looked down at my knees. Both were swollen and aching. I'd had some trouble with my right knee the year before. Twice during the year, it had clicked and swollen to twice its size. Both times, I managed to finish the event and give it rest and have the swelling come down. I knew it was a torn meniscus. I'd injured it years earlier, but it hadn't interfered with my ability to play until then. I'd never had much trouble with the left knee before. Now, they were both screaming at me.

I had two weeks to rest them before our first bonspiel. I did as suggested by the RICE acronym; rest, ice, compress, elevate. I showed up for our first game, optimistic. I stretched and warmed up like never before. I rarely used medication for any purpose. On this day, I had the maximum recommended dose of ibuprofen in me.

I was able to play, but I was in pain. By the second game, my joints were swelling again. The medication wasn't enough to control it. I felt old. I only feel old when I'm in pain. I looked around the rink. It seemed like all the other teams were made up of twelve-year-olds. They were adults, but they seemed so young. Some had man buns. Some seemed to be wearing pajamas. It saddened me to think I might have become a curmudgeon, and maybe the competitive game had just passed me by.

I made the agonizing decision to withdraw from the team. I couldn't guarantee that my body would cooperate, and if I was in pain, I was probably doing more damage to my joints. Worse than that, I wouldn't be able to perform the way I expected and at the level my team deserved. I went to the doctor already knowing the diagnosis. I would need surgery.

I had contemplated quitting several times in previous years, but not this year. I was looking forward to this year as much as any season before. I was on a good team, and I didn't have cattle. I had plenty of vacation time. But I'd gotten old. The image of all the young players kept flashing through my mind. I was thirty years older than some of them. I needed surgery as a result of the high mileage on my knees. All the signs said, "Stop."

I didn't go anywhere near a rink for four weeks. Then I went and had my lunch at the rink. My office was just a couple of blocks from the Dauphin Curling Club. It had been my routine for years to gobble my lunch, then hurry to the rink and throw about forty practice rocks. I did it even when I didn't have any events coming up. The rink air and the bit of exercise helped keep me more alert for my clients in the afternoon. One should never nod off when another is pouring his heart out.

While having lunch at the rink, it occurred to me that maybe I should go out one day and try sliding flatfoot instead of on my toe. Perhaps that would take some pressure off my knee. I had been to see the doctor and was on the list for surgery on my right knee, and the swelling in the left one was subsiding, having benefited from four weeks of rest.

I went back to the rink the next day at noon. I put my steel toe slider on as usual and added a strip of duct tape over my heel to make it slippery too. I gingerly stepped onto the ice and tried a very short, mostly upright practice slide. So far, so good. I had to protect the knee that was getting surgery, so I modified my set up. Instead of crouching in the hack and bending my knees one hundred and forty degrees, I stayed more upright, limiting the bend in my knees to thirty or forty degrees. From there, I could reach down to the handle of the rock and push forward.

    I slid only a few feet at first. I wanted to be careful not to return to balloon knees. I gradually slid a bit further and then threw a few stones.

    I got back to my office, feeling quite energized. It looked like; if I modified my delivery, I might at least be able to play recreationally again. I threw a few rocks most lunch hours for the next couple of weeks. The knees were doing okay. I began working on the adjustment to a new throwing technique. I'd spent all my life throwing from a tuck position, where most of the body's weight rides on the ball of my left foot. Throwing flatfoot changed my balance. There was more weight on my right (trailing) leg, which resulted in more rapid deceleration while sliding. It didn't seem to affect hitting as much as it did draw weight. I kept working on it.

    The annual Dauphin cash bonspiel was coming up in a week. I got the silly notion that I'd like to try my new delivery in competition. The entry date had passed, and the field was full. I thought that maybe I could hitch onto a team traveling in. Sometimes teams have a player that can't go at the last minute, so they call the bonspiel host to see if anyone local can fill in.

    I called the guy taking entries. He was somebody I knew well, a local rival. I told him I knew it was too late to enter, but did he know of anybody short a player.

    He said, "Actually, my team is. Would you like to

play with us?"

"Interesting. You heard I'm injured?"

"Yep."

"You know I changed my delivery, and I could be a bit erratic?"

"Yep."

"I don't have my usual mobility because my right leg needs surgery. So I can't sweep and need to skip?"

"Yep."

"Okay, when's our first game?"

Thus began a new team and new friendships.

We were okay in that bonspiel but not good enough to qualify for the money round. My new flatfoot delivery was steady enough, but I lacked the touch needed for the more precise draws. I was probably at least ten percent off my usual ability.

Two of my new teammates had been through the challenges of knee problems, and they'd both had the type of operation that I was scheduled to have. They suggested I talk to my doctor about a specific anti-inflammatory medication they both used. I did, and it was miraculous.

It reduced the inflammation enough that I could return to my tuck delivery. We entered zone playdowns, and it looked like we might have a realistic chance to win. We came close, losing on a fluke in the A final.

I shut myself down for the rest of the year. My surgery was to be in March. I'd have all summer to rehab. With surgery coming and my newly discovered anti-inflammatory, I felt like I might just keep curling.

The Veterans

My surgery went well, and I did my part by doing the rehab exercises and not pushing it too fast. When curling season arrived again, I felt tremendous, like the gap was closing between the pajama boys and me. My accidental team from the previous year was ready too. I was on the right team at the right time for me. I'd spent a few years connecting with people from other corners of the province. It was all great, but now I wanted to give up the chase.

Ray and Bob were Dauphin guys near the same age as me. All of us had chased the game in our younger years. We still had the appetite to compete; we just weren't going to travel all over the damn place to do it. We would enter the local super league and dominate it for several years. And we'd play a minimal number of bonspiels.

I asked an old friend from Winnipeg to join our lineup for the upcoming WCT bonspiel in Dauphin. Our lineup consisted of Bob at the lead position, Bob at second, Ray at third, and Rae at skip. How could we miss with a lineup like that? We got on a fantastic run and won the bonspiel on last rock (described in chapter one).

Ray said, "Remember when you were younger, and you played those older guys - the cagey old veterans? You could get up on the scoreboard, but they wouldn't go away. They'd just keep lobbing them in. They'd never give you anything easy. I think we've become those guys. We're Those Guys now."

It was true. We were the cagey old veterans that the young guys hated to play.

OFF THE ICE

"I may not look it when I'm playing, but I think I'm a fun guy to hang with when I'm relaxing."
David Duvall

I think many competitive players might minimize how significant downtime is to the entire experience. Downtime; it's the time before, in between, and after games. It can be the best part of a bonspiel. If you're a traveling team, it means hotel rooms and curling rink lounges. It's ordering breakfast in a small-town diner. It's driving time there and back.

I found that drives usually went quickly. There was always lots to talk about. I wish I could report that there were in-depth discussions on social issues and current events, but much of the time, a debate started with the question, who farted?

The conversation drifted into work, family, and other subjects of personal interest. One of the determinants of health is strong social connections. It's one of the things that being on a curling team gives you. Your teammates are brothers in the curling fraternity. When you change teams, you have new frat brothers. The curling community as a whole is part of a larger fraternity. When you meet somebody who says they're a curler, you know something about them already.

They know the same language as you do – the language of curling: "we lost on a pick," "it's greasy out there," "the pebble's crunchy at first but keens up by the third," "watch for fudging around the eighth." There's no translation required for curlers.

I had a teammate who said that if his car broke down in any town in Manitoba, he'd know somebody to call that would help him. The curling community includes the fans of the game, many of them former curlers themselves. Others have grown to love it from watching it on TV. I walked into a TV viewing lounge where a guy was watching a game on TV. I stopped to watch too. He made comments that suggested a reasonably high-level understanding of the game and its strategy. I said: "Ah, a curler, are you?" He said he'd never thrown a rock in his life but absolutely loved watching it on TV.

If it's been a while since the last bonspiel and your team is still on speaking terms, the anticipation of seeing them again is part of the fun. Often the kibitzing and laughing start right away. The mood is light when you get to the rink. There are light-hearted conversations with other teams just arriving. The beginning of a bonspiel is a time to be loose and enjoy your company. Nobody has lost a game. Nobody is mad, disappointed, or frustrated yet.

Card games are the most frequent post-game activity, whether in hotel rooms or the curling rink lounge. After curlers are done battling each other on the ice, they continue competing around a table. Hotly contested games of Texas Hold'em claimed more victims. There was never any money sitting on the table in these public places, of course. That would be wrong.

Dice

The game I preferred was liars dice. It only cost three loonies to play. It's a simple form of poker. Your objective was to beat the call of the player passing an inverted cup with dice underneath. If you didn't believe he had what he called, you lifted the cup to expose him as a liar. If the hand was there, or if it was better than the one called, it was you that paid. A good strategy was to take care of your neighbor, the person seated next to you. That would earn you favor with him and make him less likely to yank the cup on you. So if you needed to beat a pair of tens and rolled three queens, you might under call and say "pair of jacks." He had the choice of rolling any number of dice or simply pass the cup to his neighbor. I've seen games with numerous players around a huge banquet table, and the cup is given to player after player, with no new roll. It was high drama and laughter anytime somebody tried to expose a liar by yanking the cup.

My team was playing with people from other teams in our hotel room one night. A big part of the game is the talking, trying to gauge whether somebody is lying. My teammate was one of the masters, and I tried my best to be unpredictable. At the end of the night, one of our visitors told his roommate: "I'm not sure if those guys hate each other that much or if they were playing me, but I'm the one out of money."

On another team, we used liars dice to determine who would get the comfortable beds and who got the hide-a-beds or cots. It would be fair. Everybody had an equal chance to get a quality mattress. I never slept on a cot.

The Deer Hunter

We headed to a bonspiel in Yorkton, Saskatchewan. We had a teammate that was a hunter, and he brought his rifle with him. He bought a Saskatchewan hunting license, and between games, went hunting. He got one. He showed up just before game time with a deer in the back of the truck. We played our game. Then he took his deer to a local meat cutter. We picked it up on the way home.

The Calcutta

The calcutta auction became very popular in the eighties and continues at some events to this date. The concept is simple. Teams get auctioned off to the highest bidder. If the team you buy "places," usually first or second place in each event, you win the percentage payout assigned to that placing. An example would be a three-event bonspiel where the first and second place teams in each event produce payouts, six winners. The first place payout might be thirty percent of the total pot, with smaller percentages going to the five remaining placings.

The bidders would include the players themselves, local fans, family members, curling watchers, and a few straight-up gamblers. The teams favored to win commanded the highest bids. The odds would be good if you bought a favorite, but the payout would need to be bigger than the price paid to make a profit.

The real money is in the bargains. The trick is to find a team flying under the radar, one that you could get for a low price, and then pay off with a run to the finals. Most cheap teams are a bargain for a reason. They're longshots. An astute buyer will look for a good team that isn't well known, one that has a stronger than usual lineup for the weekend. Then he looks at the draw to see the early matchups. Maybe his horse plays a favorite in the first game. That's a better scenario than playing a weak team. When your prospect plays the big team early, it's an easier path to the finals if they win. If they lose, they drop to the second event, where they're likely to have an easier time of making the finals in that event. He may look ahead for potential second-round matchups too. Some bidders buy several teams, trying to avoid having two teams they "own" playing an elimination game.

Most teams will bid on themselves. If they're confident, it's a way to add some cash to the Mastercraft wrenches chosen from the prize table. The largest total pot in an event I've played in was in the six figures.

Snow Lake

I played in the Snow Lake Men's bonspiel one year. Snow Lake is a mining town in northern Manitoba. I went up with a teammate from Brandon, who guaranteed it would be a good time. His brother entered us under his name, thinking somebody might recognize mine. There was fierce bidding, but we managed to get our team for a bargain. The calcutta occurred after teams had played one or two games. It spread out the field and made it more possible to pick winners in each event.

My enduring impressions of Snow Lake included the fact that it had a stretcher room. I'd never been in a curling rink that had a stretcher in it. I understood why, later. I watched it be put to use several times that weekend, clearing the ice surface of collapsing drunks.

The other curious thing was the curling squirrels in the trophy case. Some local taxidermist had created a curling scene with squirrels holding mini brooms, throwing mini rocks on a mini-sheet of ice. It was impossible not to stare at it and admire the detail.

One local gambler bought several teams in the

calcutta. If they all made the finals, he could clean up. He settled in behind the glass with a cocktail to watch his teams play. He became more intoxicated the worse his teams did. That night, every team he bought got eliminated from the bonspiel. He later went home, and while going downstairs to stoke his woodstove, he fell and broke his leg. Buyer beware of the calcutta.

The bonspiel went very well for us. We won the event we were in and claimed beautiful Hudson Bay parkas as our prize. It also meant we had a sizable calcutta payout coming our way. We had to hit the road and get home, so brother Craig said he'd get the cheque and forward our share. We tried to connect with him a couple of days later. We learned he'd skipped town with our winnings. Snow Lake was everything I'd hoped for out of a northern bonspiel, good curling, wildness, big prizes, and the icing on the cake; being stiffed by our own teammate. I've never seen that money to this day.

The Eye Doctor

The Brandon Men's Bonspiel had a calcutta too. The bonspiel committee persuaded a local cattle auctioneer to conduct the bidding. What's in a name, they say. A few people have had trouble with mine over the years. Phonetically it sounds; Koo yan pa. Kujanpaa. With Scandinavian names, the j sounds like a y.

The auctioneer looked at my name and tried it a couple of times but knew it wasn't right. There was an ophthalmologist in Brandon that had a similar sounding name. The auctioneer tried again: "I don't know how to say this name, but it looks like he could be an eye doctor. How much for the eye doctor? Hundred dollars for the eye doctor?"

From that day forward, I was forever known as Eye Doctor to the people who were there. I couldn't help but smile when twenty years later, I'd walk into a rink and hear: "Eye Doctor! How are ya?"

Booze

It's not possible to talk about off-ice time without addressing alcohol use. Fortunately, or not, I had a front-row seat to the Yin and Yang of alcohol use for more than a decade. I worked in an alcohol and drug rehab center during the week and spent my weekends at curling rinks. Sometimes the contrast was too stark: similar to when you leave a thirty-degree beach in Mexico and land in thirty below temperatures in Winnipeg five hours later. It's hard to believe the two worlds can co-exist.

At work, I listened to people tearfully describe how addiction took everything they had from them; jobs, families, friendships, health, and freedom. They explained how they tried to cover the problem by hiding it from everybody. They believed nobody knew how much they really drank. They described how their disease hid its presence from them like a hidden parasite; and how humbling it was to come to terms with how much devastation they caused to others' lives. For them, there was no safe amount of alcohol.

Then I went to the rink. For some teams arriving, the first drinks of the weekend were already consumed. Some went to the bar before looking at the draw. Occasionally, somebody would get there intoxicated.

It should be made clear that for the majority of curlers, drinking was not a problem. A priest (father Martin) known for his work with alcoholics, noted that for many people, alcohol was something that could enhance a social experience, "The gift from God that gladdens the heart." And so it was for some, but not all.

I painted houses and fences one summer. I saw peeling paint everywhere after that. I saw fences and homes that needed work when I'd never noticed that before my painting job. When I walked out the doors of the rehab center after a shift, I saw a river of alcohol pouring through the lives of people everywhere. I tried to look away. I tried to keep the two worlds separate. Curling time was my time, when I could get away from the pain and emotion of working with people who've been unwittingly damaged by something. Yet, I saw alcohol problems whether I tried to see them or not.

Some people knew where I worked and seemed uncomfortable, as if I might know something about them. I wished that wasn't true. I sometimes said, "Relax, I'm off duty." I wanted to assure them that I knew that this weekend was their time off too, and that there was nothing wrong with enjoying a few drinks with friends. I wanted to assure them that even occasional intoxication did not, in itself, indicate the presence of a problem. Most of all, I didn't want to talk about it at all. It was my day off.

Invariably, people waited until they were severely intoxicated before they wanted to talk about their problem. Drunks never realize they don't have the capacity to solve problems when intoxicated. I'd give them my number and invite them to call tomorrow or anytime after that. They never called. As part of my job, I got calls from the hospital to come and assess patients who'd been admitted for detox. Some of them were curlers.

The stories involving alcohol and curling are numerous. Many of them are hilarious. I wish those were the only ones I knew.

The Roller Coaster

I made two more career changes late in my working years. I feared complacency and declining effectiveness after two decades in addictions. I watched a counselor become burned out near the end of their career. I wanted to avoid a similar fate.

I had taken my turn on the executive of our union's local and participated as a member rep on our bargaining committee. I caught the attention of some of the union's leadership. They suggested I consider applying for an upcoming vacancy in Dauphin for a staff position. It was a tough decision. I loved my counseling job, but could I sustain my professionalism for another five to ten years before considering retiring? It was a dilemma; play it safe or get back on the roller coaster.

I did my due diligence. I interviewed several union staff about the nature of the work and whether it was a fit for me. One person gave an answer that would ring in my ears for years to follow. "There's not a lot of appreciation for the work we do."

I got on the roller coaster, and once again, found myself staring up the slope of a steep learning curve. There was no easing-in period. I found myself needing to be conversant in labor law, human rights legislation, employment standards, twenty-five different collective agreements, and more. The vast majority of the people I served did an excellent job for fair-minded managers. They efficiently resolved any workplace issues. Those were not the files that came over my desk.

Two of us served over two thousand members within twenty-five different bargaining units. In addition to running around as a labor firefighter, I became the lead negotiator for bargaining several local collective agreements. I'd hoped not to coast into retirement. I got my wish.

After five years of frantic service, I moved on again. This time, I took a term as an instructor at the local community college. It was an essential skills and employment readiness program. I've sometimes explained that my life has been a series of totally unrelated events.

In reality, it seems like previous experiences positioned me uniquely for the next thing. I stood in front of a class struggling on the margins of employability. Some of their barriers included understanding their rights as employees versus their obligations to expectant employers. Some struggled with substance abuse or mental health issues. Some simply needed a little boost to any academic shortcomings.

I started a business, offering my services as a workplace consultant. I continued with the college for other targeted training programs, like a pre-college essential skills course. I contracted with another agency to do more targeted workplace training programs, including things like respectful workplace issues and diversity in the workplace.

It had been a tough decision to leave the familiarity of a field where I'd grown comfortable. The experiences that came after counseling added new ingredients to my work-life soup. I made the right choice.

RIVALRIES

"Believe me, the reward is not so
great without the struggle."
Wilma Rudolph

In 2012, the format for entry into provincials had changed. Larger sport regions replaced the many zones that existed before. Our sport region had two provincial berths available. Our team was positioned to do well. We had the highest number of total wins in the previous two years of Parkland Super League curling. We were regularly seeded number one or two going into play-downs each year.

The players did the seeding. Entries were received centrally by the MCA in Winnipeg; then, the MCA sent a list of the teams to all the entries for seeding. It was a system that generally worked well. People in their regions knew how to rank their opponents. The top teams tended to be the top teams every year. The order changed slightly based on recent successes, but it was always clear who the top three or four teams were.

But 2012 was different. Beautiful Credit Union Place in Dauphin was hosting the provincials. Every curler in the Parkland region wanted to be the home team at this made-for-curling venue. The show was coming to Dauphin.

There was a bit more tension among the usual rivalries in the weeks leading up to regionals. Everybody wanted to play in the home arena. The same teams battled it out every year, in super league, in bonspiels, and regionals. There was a high degree of familiarity among the players, and generally, the same teams beat the same teams most of the time.

The draw for regionals was released a few days before the competition began. It instantly raised some eyebrows. Two of the top three teams were to play each other in the first round, with the winner playing us in the second round. The winner of that game would play the fourth-best team in the field. It was clear that some seeding tinkering had gone on. The top three teams were clustered on the long side of the draw.

Several lower end teams had colluded to upset the usual seeding pattern. They had not been very discreet about it, and somehow it worked. All of the perennial top seeds were on one side of the draw, and the lower-ranked teams just had to battle each other to reach the A-side final.

One might argue that seeding doesn't matter, that you need to emerge from the field no matter what order you play teams. It is true that the best teams often battle it out at the end. It's actually more a benefit to the lower-ranked squad to have the draw out of whack. If the seeding were true to form, the last ranked team would play the best team in their first game, a tough match-up. If they win that game, the low seed then plays the fourth seed in the semi-final and either the number two or three seed in the final.

When the seeding is right, the last ranked team has to beat three of the top four seeds. In the draw we saw in 2012, the low ranked team didn't have to worry about a top seed until the finals. And anything can happen in one game.

The regionals were being hosted in Swan River that year. I remember walking into the rink and feeling the tension. None of the top seeds were happy. The colluding teams were quiet: it was not clear how many of them had contributed to the master plan. The usual pre-event banter was stilted.

We had a brief conversation with a couple of the other top teams. It was clear there was nothing we could do. The players do the seeding, and they are responsible for the integrity of the process. The final statement was still going to be made on the ice.

In the first round, the third-best team in the field beat the second best. In the second round, we beat them. Just like that, two of the three top teams were on the B side. Adding to the prickly dynamics that weekend was that many players from various teams had played as teammates before. There was unsettling familiarity within the field. You just know how somebody is thinking and reacting if you've been on the same team with them.

We played the fourth-best team in the A-side semi-final. They seemed uptight. I'm not sure if they were annoyed that they were victims of the seeding coup or upset that it backfired on themselves. I've never asked the question, and an answer was never offered.

The game was a battle. They had us in big trouble a couple of times, but I managed to use the out-shot left to us to escape. They had an opportunity to put a boot on our throats in the seventh end and missed. It left me an open draw.

I slid out of the hack. While in the process of putting the turn on the handle of the stone, I heard a loud smack. Debris showered the ice in front of my rock. My sweepers frantically leaped into action to clear the debris away from the path. They did a good job; I made my shot.

One of our opponents had smashed his sliding device on the bench and shattered it. That's what had caused the plastic rainstorm. I looked toward the bench and fired a laser glare, intended to burn a hole in the body of the lead, the one I thought was responsible for the outburst. His eyes broke away from the assault. My third turned on their third to protest what had happened. Their third was apologetic and did not defend his player's actions. Their skip, the actual perpetrator of the crime, remained at the other end by himself.

It had been a heck of a day, but now we were in the A final—one more bit of business to finish. We were pretty punchy going into that final. Our opponent was the fifth-best team in the field and had a leisurely ride through the lesser ranked teams. They seized their opportunity and were excited to be playing in an A final, if not a bit surprised. Besides, there were some personality differences between our teams. We didn't enjoy playing them. It would have to be all business.

The game was a grind. The antagonists played well, buoyed by the excitement of being in the finals. We took a workman-like approach and methodically put ourselves in a position to win. We were one up playing the tenth end with the hammer. I had a draw to the full eight-foot to seal the deal. It was all good upon release, swept lightly off and on. As it approached the top of the house, it died, as if it had entered a puddle of mud. It had caught us by surprise. We weren't even sweeping it, thinking it had enough weight to get to the tee line. No problem. These things happen. We'd still have the hammer in the extra end.

We played a perfect extra end. I had a similar-looking shot for the win once and for all; an in-turn draw to the eight-foot circle. This time when I released, the sweepers swept the whole way lightly. They weren't going to let a bit of debris decide this game. Then, my rock took a sharp right turn. Despite the fact the sweepers were cleaning the path, my rock had picked.

Game over, we lost.

I walked into the locker room and changed in silence. My third gently asked if I was "coming up?" He was asking if I wanted to go up to the lounge for a beer before we went back to our hotel. I said, "Go ahead. I'm going for a walk. I'll meet you back at the hotel." Anybody who knows me will recognize this as a major meltdown for me, as bad as it gets. And so I walked. I thought about how rare it was to have a rock "pick" when it's the game-winning shot. I'd never seen two picks on two consecutive game-winning attempts. The odds of that must be off the charts. It was like there was only one card in a stack of hundreds of cards that could beat you, and that one came up. Clearly, the curling gods had decided the outcome. I wondered what I was to think of that.

It was snowing lightly. The street lights barely illuminated my path. I stomped through cold, snowy darkness, which matched my mood perfectly. I stopped at a convenience store and grabbed a pop and some snacks. I got back to the hotel before my team and went to bed before they got back. We had lost a curling game, but we were still alive on the B side. We would have to play the best team left in the event, in our first game. Before falling asleep, I thought it might be my last competitive game. I wasn't sure I had the appetite for the ups and downs curling imposed anymore. At that moment, it seemed there were more downs than ups.

My team looked at me, apprehensively when I

emerged from my room. I realized I hadn't spoken to them since I walked off the ice. I hadn't participated in the necessary team debrief where we would correctly conclude that we'd played impressively but for a couple of unforeseen divine interventions. One of them said: "You alright? We're still in this, you know." I said: "I'm fine. I'm good to go." I made sure they knew I wasn't the least bit upset with them. They had nothing to do with my reaction to the loss.

I had decided that if this was to be my last game, I needed to make it a good one. I owed it to my team and myself. Win or lose; I wanted to feel good about how I played in my last game. I spent the morning trying to get my mind right, to put the previous day behind me and focus on the game in front of us. The team we were playing had been on a roll since dropping to the B side. They had momentum, and we were coming off a painful loss. A further complication was the fact we'd be playing four players whom I respected very much. I had played with all of them at various times and knew them to be good people, good players, and mentally resilient. Nothing would be straightforward about this.

The game turned out to be everything a curling game should be. It was well played; good strategy and good execution by both teams. Grudging respect and edginess throughout. I had to draw through a narrow port to corner freeze their counter near the button in the last end. We made the shot with the right weight, line calling, and sweeping; a team shot if ever there was one. Checkmate; our opponent had nothing. We were going to the B final.

Our opponent in the final featured a couple of ageless veterans, still competitive and determined not to be generous. They had a younger front end. The lead had never won anything but had lots to say. We approached the game workman-like again. It was the only formula this team knew. We had control of the game throughout, but it wasn't easy. It shouldn't be easy. We won. We were going to play in the provincials in Dauphin's beautiful arena after all. My retirement from competitive curling would have to wait.

The Agreement

My description of that cold weekend in January in Swan River is not meant to make the case that curling in a low-level competition in the middle of nowhere isn't worth it. Or that it isn't fun if it becomes unpleasant. Or that bad people are playing the game. It's just the opposite!

I'm eternally grateful to all the people involved with that weekend. A curling game is just a curling game, at any level, unless the two teams that play the game decide it's important. If every team entered into the competition agree the games are meaningful, they are. If the radio station and its listeners; the newspaper and its readers agree the event has value, then it has. The participants' behavior in that event in Swan River, including my own, can be questioned. But what can't be questioned is the agreement, to a man, that those games were important.

The Brier final is just a curling game. It takes the agreement of many people to make it as big as it is: the thousands who tried and failed to get there, the media, the sponsors, the thousands seated in the arena, and the millions watching on TV. It's just a game without that agreement.

A global pandemic has forced us to re-evaluate all that is important in life. It's made some of us look at the role of sports in our lives. Teams qualifying for the Stanley Cup playoffs played in empty arenas. The games were still important, made so by the players, owners, media, and fans who bothered to watch the games on TV. But the hard-fought matches missed the fans' real-time involvement, crammed into seats, cheering their approval or disapproval. The event missed the people collecting on adjacent streets, watching on big screens, and bringing energy to their city. The games were a little less critical without that.

I'm a fan of professional hockey and football. My conclusion is that I could probably live without professional sports to view from afar. It would be much harder to give up my own participation in sports. I can take a pass on watching golf on TV, but a round of my own, with ten-cent snips riding on every putt, and in the company of good people. No way.

My personal involvement with sport has evolved. A passion for water skiing has given way to windsurfing, and tennis, by necessity, has morphed into pickleball. It's hard to imagine ever reaching an age where I'd choose to be idle.

Playing Hard

The cold battles we have on the ice raise other questions. How important is winning? What ethical line are you willing to cross to get there? Is simply winning more important than how you won? These questions aren't for the small number who are absolutely pure of heart. They're for the rest of us. Is there any harm in messing with the seeding of the draw? It didn't affect the outcome of any actual games. Did it change the integrity of the event?

If you have information that gives you an advantage, would you share it? An example is knowing something about a set of rocks. Some rocks in the set curl more than others. You may say that doing the work of understanding rocks is part of your own team's preparation, and your opponents should do the same. You wouldn't expect them to share that information with you if they had it.

What about giving false information? If the bad guys miss a shot, you say: "Oh, that was the number five rock. It cuts way more than the six." In reality, your team has determined the number six rock curls more. Are we at your line yet?

Is there anything wrong with standing at the hogline to monitor the thrower to make sure he doesn't cross it? Does it matter that you haven't been there the whole game, but it's now the game-winning shot attempt? Is there anything wrong with adopting a demeanor that an opponent might find unsettling or distracting: unfriendly, aloof, overly friendly, chatty, angry, indignant?

So far, everything described is often defined within the broad category of gamesmanship. Many would say gamesmanship is to be expected and within the acceptable parameters of the game. It's not overt cheating, even if it's not genuinely sportsmanlike. Still pure of heart? Gamesmanship takes many forms in curling. Sometimes it's mean-spirited, and other times it's just taking advantage of an opportunity to catch an opponent not paying attention. It was hard to mount a comeback in the days before the free guard zone rule was introduced. The team with the lead would peel guard after guard unless there were an opportunity to add to their point total.

We were two down in a Westman Super League game being played on a frosty night in Wawanesa. We had the hammer and tried to play corner guards. They peeled every one of them. Playing into the house late in an end signals your acceptance that you can't score a deuce, and you're ready to move on to the next end.

My skip called for me to draw to the four foot. Before I went to deliver my rock, he whispered, "Drop it about fifteen feet short and give me a performance." I understood. I threw it too lightly, then implored my sweepers to save me by sweeping with all they had. The rock came to a stop halfway between the hog line and house. I smacked the ice with my broom, hung my head, and muttered something.

This bit of acting was one version of the broken wing strategy. The other team now had a perfect center guard and an apparently frustrated opponent who'd lost draw weight. They had a short discussion and decided to go for our throats. They drew around the center guard but were fooled by my light throw. Their rock came too deep, to the back of the button, and I promptly froze onto it. The skip had played hits to defend his lead and now had to freeze to mine on the button to save the end. He, too, was about two feet heavy.

His stone gently bounced off and sat beside mine. My skip drew another counter next to mine. Our opponent, now rattled, had to make a perfect shot just to limit us to two. It was not good enough, and we drew in for a count of three; all three were biting the button. No words needed to be spoken. They knew they'd just been victims of one of the oldest tricks in the book, the broken wing.

I learned a hard lesson when I lost the Brandon zone final in 1987. I stopped trusting my instincts at a crucial moment, with the game on the line. I put my broom down in the same spot my opponent had, despite my gut telling me I needed more ice. I should have trusted my gut, something I tried to do from that point forth.

I also knew that if I blinked in a moment of self-doubt, others might too. When I later became the name to beat in zone play-downs, I knew I could occasionally goad lesser teams into mistakes. It's something that couldn't be done too often or be too obvious. But once in a while, I'd catch an opponent stealing my ice and not trusting their own ice reading. At the right moment, I'd put the broom down six inches tighter than required, then use my third's leg as the target. If my opponent didn't watch me throw or didn't trust his eyes, he'd take the tight ice and wrack on the guard.

Broomgate

Elite players work harder than the rest of us. They work out, practice, and plan. They test throwing and sweeping techniques while the wannabes watch hockey on TV. Elite teams discovered the effects of directional sweeping as a way to manipulate the path of the rock. Some of the world's best teams were responsible for a controversy that came to a head in 2015. The fabrics used on their brooms became more coarse and firm. It created a sandpaper effect that would guide the direction of the rock when combined with directional sweeping. It became less important to throw the rock accurately. Directional sweeping would manipulate the stone onto the correct path. Shooting percentages went up through the roof.

But not every team used these aggressive materials. Some were beholden to sponsors that didn't have an equivalent product. Some chose not to use them on principle.

There was nothing in the rule book that prevented the use of these brooms. But it affected the integrity of the competition. A guiding principle in sport is that everybody is on an equal playing field, and the skill and athleticism of the participants would determine the outcome.

The brooms tilted the field. Imagine two professional hockey teams where one team has high-grade composite sticks, and the other has straight wooden Victoriavilles, like the ones I used to buy at the grocery in town for $1.99.

The World Curling Federation banned the controversial broom heads for the 2015/2016 season. An approved fabric was made available to all major manufacturers, and broom compliance checks became standard before and during all competitive play.

Again, before the ban, nobody broke any written rules. There are other behaviors to contemplate, like the high profile team coercing an ice maker to create conditions they prefer. A version of "working the refs."

There have been cases of sabotage, like hiding a piece of equipment belonging to an opponent. Is this all still fair game? Where did we cross your line?... or are we not there yet?

One of the risks we run when we decide a game is important is to compromise our integrity. It's easy to remove a burned rock that nobody saw in a club game. Can you do it in the big one? That's a situation addressed in the comedy film "Men With Brooms." On the final shot thrown by Chris, Eddie burns the rock, and Chris sees it. Chris reports the foul to the official. In the real world, he would have lost the final on a burned rock. In movie world, his opponent Yount is so impressed with Chris's honesty that he allows a re-shot that Chris then dramatically makes. Only in the movies.

Curling and winning are important. How important?

THE MCA

"It's a routine many curlers have followed. The Saturday before the MCA bonspiel, you wake up and go straight to the mailbox. The hash browns and eggs will have to wait. You need to check the draw in the Winnipeg Free Press.

Scanning through all the names, you're eager to see your first match-up. Maybe it's against your neighbor, your MLA, or an old pal from high school. Perhaps you've hit the jackpot and have drawn a Canadian champion. You put down your coffee and spread the news to your friends. This is your chance to shine at the world's largest bonspiel."

Sean Grassie

The above is an excerpt from the book "Kings of the Rings" by Sean Grassie. In it, he chronicles the storied history of this fantastic curling phenomenon. It has been the centerpiece of Manitoba curling since 1889. Grassie tells of a letter written by Hugh Cowan in 1902. Cowan was a Scot who traveled to Winnipeg to play in the MCA and reported his findings to The Scotsman, a newspaper back home. "The Winnipeg air is crisp. Shops are decorated, flags are flying, and hotels are packed. Visitors have come from Edmonton, Duluth, St Paul, and the Yukon. The streets are full of men with brooms in their hands."

Manitoba curling legends have cemented their place in history with their well documented MCA performances. For many more, it was a great way to spend a week with three good curling buddies.

My first MCA was the bonspiel's one hundredth. Entries had been steadily rising and had to be capped at eight hundred forty-eight in the eighties. For the one-hundredth anniversary, the MCA took twelve hundred and eighty teams. Those foursomes played on one hundred eighty-seven sheets of ice throughout Winnipeg and a few nearby towns. The games began Wednesday morning, and the bonspiel didn't conclude until Wednesday evening, the following week.

The week started with a trip to the International Inn to pick up our bonspiel package. The essential thing in the envelope for a rural team was the map of Winnipeg that included directions to the various curling clubs spread evenly throughout the city. Winnipeg's founders built it around the intersection of two meandering rivers. There's no perfect grid pattern of streets and avenues. The first time through Winnipeg's infamous "confusion corner" is a real treat for a country boy. It's also important to know that the

Valour Road Curling club isn't actually on the street named Valour Road.

Our bonspiel package also contained our banquet ticket. It is an MCA tradition to provide a large smorgasbord meal at the International Inn banquet room. Warmers provided unlimited portions over two days. Curlers scarfed down five thousand meals; volunteers, sponsors, and media consumed another thousand.

Organizers kept the draw in a conference room in the same hotel. There were several long aisles with tripods supporting sections of draw sheets, which would form the complete draw if stacked one upon another. I enjoyed trying to find my name on the draw. Volunteers sat behind banks of phones. Umpires from various clubs called in the results after every round; the volunteers physically wrote the results onto the draw sheets. All twelve hundred and eighty teams would then call headquarters to ask the location of their next game.

I marveled at the logistical nightmare that organizers overcame to make the bonspiel run. I guess one hundred years of steady bonspiel growth taught the lessons needed to pull it off. I couldn't help but be impressed by the magnitude of the event. There were teams from Europe in the field. There were Americans, and there were Canadians from most provinces. The majority of teams belonged to city clubs, but the MCA reserved four hundred spots for rural teams like mine. The bonspiel showcased the depth of Manitoba curling during those years.

The bonspiel was great and exhausting. In this, my first MCA bonspiel, I had no idea where we were on the draw or in the city. I remember being on the ice in ten or eleven different clubs and always driving in the dark looking for the club that would host our next game.

The format of the bonspiel was quite incredible too. There were two main events, meaning you played on two parallel draws of 1280 teams on alternating draw times. It was, in effect, playing in two massive bonspiels at the same time. Both main events had numerous minor events below it, should you lose a game or several games. Everybody in the bonspiel was guaranteed a minimum of eight games. The first six games served the purpose of sorting teams among the major and minor events. After that, a loss on either side of the concurrent bonspiels would eliminate you from that side. If you could manage to put eleven hundred and seventy-six teams behind you in a major event, you won a berth into the Manitoba provincial championship. Good luck to everybody!

I played in a total of nine MCA's over the years and witnessed changes over that time. It inevitably got a little smaller. My first experience impressed me with the sheer scale of the event. Later, I got a better feel for how we were doing. If we won a few games in a major event, I could calculate how far we were from one of the coveted semi-final spots.

I offer this as an observation rather than an

excuse. All things being equal, it's harder to do well as a beyond-the-perimeter team. Even if a team is reasonably well behaved, it's still; seven nights in a strange bed, long hours with little downtime, and over-stimulation. I suspect city players slipped home for a bit of couch time while we played cards in yet another curling club dining area.

I've played in the bonspiel with a trip to provincials already secured, and other times, I hoped to be one of the few who got a spot through the bonspiel. Either way, the MCA is a bonspiel to be experienced and not just for the curling. There's so much going on. Curlers knew many clubs for specialties served in their kitchens. We couldn't wait for Fort Rouge pizza, the soup at Pembina, and greasy burgers at the Thistle.

One year I discovered an annual MCA tradition at the Granite, the Motherclub, founded in 1880. It happens in the second-floor lounge, a sing-a-long party. There's a piano in the lounge on one side, and a few people bring guitars. One of the party organizers brought overheads with the lyrics to the songs to illuminate a wall and encourage the shy to sing too.

It's an excellent room for a party, with a glass trophy case containing the original "Silver Broom," the now-retired trophy that had been presented to world champions. The space includes the best table in curling, as dubbed by a teammate. It was a corner table with large glass windows overlooking illuminated river walking trails and Manitoba's legislative building.

The piano player had the apt nickname "Middle C." Middle C asked me where I was from. I told him Rorketon and prepared to give my usual shpiel about where that was. He said: "I know where that is. I'm coming to the men's bonspiel up there next month." Sure.

A month later, I walked into the lobby of the Rorketon Curling Club and saw Middle C. He had a buddy from Meadow Portage, just up the road from Rorketon. Curling is like that.

The MCA is played in the third week of January, statistically the coldest week of the year in Manitoba. Some years we couldn't keep enough washer fluid to keep the windows clean on the slushy streets. Other years it was cold- frigid. The worst in memory was when the province set a record for the longest number of consecutive days where the daytime high temperature did not exceed minus thirty Celsius. That streak included the entire MCA bonspiel. Our van was pretty good, but we didn't take chances. We could leave it in the parking lot for the duration of the game but no longer. Right after the game, somebody would run out to start it and run it a while. Even so, we required a boost once. It was a common sight in the rink parking lots; curlers boosting each other's vehicles. Some people let their cars run throughout to keep them from freezing up.

I enjoyed it every time I played it. We had some excellent runs. We twice lost the game that would have given us a provincial spot. We lost the game that would have got us into the game for a berth. There was the "cash over badges game."

A first-place finish was the best performance I ever experienced. In my last MCA bonspiel, we cleared the field and won a major event. The winner of the parallel major was a former world champion. We got a picture with the big trophy for the MCA yearbook and got keeper plaques in the shape of the province of Manitoba. I hold it as one of my favorite possessions because of the beautiful history of the MCA bonspiel. It's like Disneyland for curlers.

THE STATE OF THE GAME

> "Statistics are like bikinis-they show a lot but not everything."
> *Lou Piniella*

A ten-year-old version of myself, throwing his first curling rock today, would have a far different path forward than I did back in the seventies. The game: the ice, rocks, rules, equipment, opportunities, and world have all changed. It's not useful to long for bygone days. There are a few old-timers living in small communities who fondly remember a farm family on every quarter section. Those days are gone.

Gone too are the days when a curler could have it both ways; one foot in competitive curling and the other, fully out. Some years, I barely had a toe in competitive curling, but it wasn't unreasonable to dip just a toe. It was possible for four buddies to hop into a vehicle, drive a few hours, and play Canadian champions. It was possible to compete with them, even if the percentage of wins against those teams wasn't impressive.

My curling career has spanned nearly a half-century, starting in 1971—what a time to be alive and bear witness to the game's rapid evolution. There were absolutely no people in the world who listed Curler as their occupation. There was far more time spent in snake pits than in gyms.

The Elites

The elite teams were right to boycott two consecutive Briers to advance their cause. They were right to form Grand Slam events, played in arenas around the country, for only the best teams. They were right to pressure provincial and national curling associations to further their own competitive interests. They were right because the results speak for themselves. At the elite level, the game has evolved to new heights. Canadian teams have had to work hard to maintain their place atop the curling world. International teams continue to work harder and develop their game (with the help of Canadian coaches).

Canadian teams continue to be the ones to beat entering any international competition. The changes of the last twenty years helped ensure this. Elite teams now play a large number of their games on arena ice. Arena ice is different, and all the most significant championships are played in arenas. High ranking teams qualify for government sport funding as a result of curling's inclusion in the Olympics. That, together with increased prize money and sponsorship, created the conditions for curling professionals.

The elite teams built a firewall between themselves and all the teams below them. Entry into Grand Slam events is only available to a handful of teams in the world. It works. Hundreds of thousands of TV viewers cheer their favorite teams in the finals each week. They holler at their screens at the same people playing the same people week after week. The firewall had an unintended consequence. How would this pool of immense talent be replenished?

On the farm, we'd excavate a dugout to provide water for the cattle. But if we didn't contemplate how more water would replenish the dugout, it would go dry. A healthy pool needs renewal. The elites' interests were self-serving, creating conditions to advance their standing, but they didn't anticipate how they would replace themselves. Only eighteen teams played in Grand Slam events, and a big steel fence surrounded them.

The new curling stratosphere was inarguably good for the forward progress of the high-level game. It's questionable whether it was healthy for the game overall. The Slam brain trust recognized the problem they had created and responded with the introduction of a tier two event running concurrently with Slam events. Sixteen teams would play in this event.

That didn't fully solve the problem. The tier two teams in Slam events weren't really tier two. They were the bottom half of tier one. To participate regularly in these events, a team had to follow the Slams throughout the country. It meant lots of travel and expense and playing for less money. Playing in these events required a significant amount of cash and commitment, not unlike the original eighteen. There is a very narrow pathway for anybody aspiring to play at the highest level.

The pathway begins at a young age. If you have a coach, play in provincials and get high-performance training, you are on the path. If you are not on one of the top four teams in the province by the end of your junior years, you are probably off the path. If you go to university and take a full course load or work full time, you are probably off the track. Elite curling has more rewards than ever and requires more sacrifice than ever.

For the university student, some tough choices apply. Taking a reduced course load enables daily training sessions and the extended weekends needed to compete. But taking a reduced course load increases the likelihood of not finishing a degree. Extending the completion date of a degree by a couple of years means sacrificing significant earning potential during that time. In many fields, a young employee needs to "pay his dues" to advance into the most desirable positions. It takes a very understanding employer to accept two or three day work weeks during the curling season. An aspiring curler sacrifices significant earning potential to chase the dream.

There's getting to be more money available for the top teams, but you don't have to go too far down the money list to see earnings that don't support the effort. The twentieth ranked golfer in the world is a multi-millionaire. The twentieth ranked curling team needs to be back on the job Monday morning. The top teams in the world get no criticism here. They have not only trained hard to be as good as they are, but they've also sacrificed a lot on the road not traveled.

The Brier

The new competitive world order has caused a problem for the Brier too. While there's always been some separation between provinces before, the gap has become a chasm. Teams still wear their provincial colors at the Brier, but realistically, there should be only two kinds of sweaters, pros and joes, because the Brier has become an event that matches pros with average joes. The average joes are all gone by the final round when the pros play for the title.

The top teams are formed of combinations from all over Canada. If you plan to win gold for Canada, why shouldn't you take the player that best fits your team, even if he lives across the country in another province? But should he wear green if he's not from Saskatchewan, or the coveted "buffalo" if he's not from

Manitoba?

So we have these super-teams in the Brier, wearing provincial colors that don't match their addresses. And we have the guys that play a couple of nights a week, got on a run, and made it to the Brier. It's embarrassing. We see scores of thirteen to one, terribly one-sided games. Fans travel from all over Canada to attend the Brier experience. They wave provincial flags and wear funny hats. They make signs and ring bells. Then they look down onto the ice and see somebody from another province wearing their colors. Or worse, they valiantly cheer on their over-matched joes against a team of unyielding pros. No chance.

The solutions are not clear. Fans of the game want to see the best teams. They provide the most entertaining games. But is the Brier still really a national championship? There are more questions than answers here. Other sports have national amateur championships. What would a Brier look like if the participants had to provide driver's licenses and street addresses from the provinces they represent? Do Slam teams, who aspire to Olympic glory, still need the Brier? Does the Brier need them? ...and does the team that represents Canada at the worlds need to come from the Brier?

The Card

My description of the top teams in Canada as elite is not intended to be any sort of condemnation. They've embraced the term themselves and even have an event they call the "Elite 10." It's working for them. But the consequence of this elitism, intended or otherwise, is the near extinction of the true tier two competitive curler—my people.

In "The Brier," published in 1995, author Bob Weeks states: "Close to 50,000 men will begin play, but only four will stand atop the podium in early March, a golden tankard held high above their heads. Along the way, dreams will die and hearts will break. A wick here and a rub there will send one team to the next game and another to the sidelines, there to wait for next year, when the dream can start all over again."

Those 50,000 men all reached into their wallets and coughed up the annual cost of the card. The Canadian Curling Association (CCA) competitor card was one of the conditions for entry into play-downs that ultimately led to the Brier. By purchasing a competitor card, you counted yourself among the thousands standing at the starting line, ready to begin the chase toward the podium. With a card in your wallet, you distinguished yourself from the many thousands of curlers who chose not to compete against the best in the game.

Various provinces have different paths to their provincial championships, including stages through the club, zone, or regional competition. Merely getting to provincials could be considered a significant achievement. It represented one percent of all competitive curlers.

The top teams are better than ever. Strangely, it's a

lot easier to get into provincials now than it used to be. In Manitoba, returning champions and top money winners receive automatic entry into provincials, so other teams never have to play them on the road to provincials. And entries are down, way down. Curling is a game that was driven by large numbers of boomers who are too old to continue competitively. Younger teams, seeing what it takes to compete at the highest levels, are opting out. The thinking is, why should one bother to go to the trouble of getting to provincials, paying for a hotel and tickets for your family, only to get slaughtered by a Slam team.

There are players out there who would like to compete. They want to preserve their full-time jobs and most of their family time. They don't aspire to the Olympics and don't care to make the commitment it would take. But they would throw a few practice rocks, travel within driving distance, and play for some money. What's left for them? Not much.

No Man's Land

The Dominion Curling Club Championship was established to provide an opportunity for club curlers to compete at a provincial and national level. The virtuous goal was to let regular club curlers in on the fun of playing against people from other parts of the province or country. In reality, the teams that won were often of competitive pedigree. The spirit of the rules was gamed. The rules were designed to eliminate competitive teams from contaminating the event so that the bonafide Tuesday night curler could compete. There were rules restricting players who had recently played in regular men's provincials or super leagues.

My team played in a super league but hadn't been to provincials for a couple of years. We weren't good enough to go to the Brier and too good to play in the Dominion. Is there something for the tier two-player, the guys who used to buy competitor cards?

The Business of Curling

There was a time when curling clubs didn't have to worry about their business. All the leagues filled up and had waiting lists. Casual renters filled the remaining time slots. There was no need for outreach to attract new people to the game. Then gradually, it changed. Leagues had openings, bonspiels didn't fill, and rinks started to close.

There continue to be many honest, hardworking club executives and other volunteers doing some innovative things to keep curling clubs viable. New members of curling clubs used to be the sons and daughters of curlers. There are fewer curlers and fewer sons and daughters choosing the game. What needs to happen to grow the game again?

If you walk into a typical curling club, you might see a long line of portraits of past curling club presidents, one old white face after another. It's changing, but we can do better. Curling clubs have long been very white, with people of color being under-represented.

Our clubs should look like our communities. If they don't, we're missing out on sharing this great game with much of our neighborhood. On this point, I hope we agree. The challenge is how to do this.

In my home town of Rorketon, curling is in the community's DNA. There are few who've never tried it, and probably nobody that doesn't know the basics of how the game is played. Yet even in Rorketon, the number of entries into a bonspiel correlates with the number of people willing to play the position of skip. Some people have curled for twenty years, but if a skip doesn't phone them and invite them to play on their team, they sit at home. Ten skips – ten teams. There might be a hundred people who would say yes to an invitation to play, but only forty will if there are just ten skips.

Knowing what the various chess pieces do doesn't make you a master chess player, but it does enable you to play a game. In curling, if you know the difference between in-turn and an out-turn, and if you know that a draw curls more than a hit, you can be a skip. It doesn't need to be intimidating.

So you've just done a curling clinic for new Canadians. It was a hit. They love it. Now, is anybody planning to call them and invite them to play on their team? One under-sourced resource every club has is its existing members. They can be skips. Track the names and contact information of casual renters and clinic participants and invite them back. It's more fun for a beginner if somebody on the team knows how to skip.

We can organize skipping clinics specifically for recreational players. Find ways to have beginners take a turn at skipping. I think we have to be open-minded about how we structure games. They can be shorter, and beginner leagues can be of a shorter duration – sign up for a month of curling, four games.

Let's remember, not everybody wants to play for participation ribbons. Keeping score and playing in a competition is what will bring some people back. Coming back to secure victory in a game that seemed lost will get their juices going. They'll tell the story in the lounge after the game and at work the next day.

Our bonspiels in Rorketon, like everywhere, used to reward only the highest finishers. We changed that by offering small prizes for every win, usually ten dollars. If you won just one game, you got something. If there were kids on the team, that ten dollars came back to the club over the kitchen and candy counter. If adults were part of the team's ingredients, we got the money back in the bar. Win-win.

I know a lot of terrible golfers who love to play nonetheless. I'm one of them. Let's never allow a curler to think they're not good enough to play in our bonspiels and leagues.

I know there are clubs all over Canada who are using some of these and many more ideas. I tip my hat to you. Curling, like many things, is best shared with others.

THE EXPERIENCE

"The suspense is terrible. I hope it will last"
Oscar Wilde

A somewhat cynical and straightforward notion of happiness is that happiness is merely experiencing a range of biochemical sensations. This is the idea advanced by Yuval Harari in his book "Sapiens: A Brief History of Humankind." I'd rather cling to the thought that there's much more to it than that. Without conceding that Harari is right, it is useful to look at what happens in the brain when we play sports.

I've been asked, "I can see how your body can be addicted to alcohol or drugs because you're putting something into your body, but how do you get addicted to a behavior?" The short answer is – because it's mood-altering. It makes you feel different. Typical behavioral (process) addictions are gambling, sex, shopping, gaming, and exercise. These are all behaviors that can enhance life experience in a healthy way. The problems happen when the actions become compulsive.

Let's be clear. Mood altering behavior is something we all do. So let there be no judgment of anybody pursuing an activity that makes them feel something. Going for a walk, watching a movie, or a home DIY project can all qualify as mood-altering behaviors. The word addiction, I think, is overused. I hear people say things like, "I have an Oreo cookie addiction." No, it may be a strong preference, and you might give yourself a stomach ache, but it's not an addiction. Those statements serve to diminish the reality experienced by those who suffer from an actual addiction.

Addiction happens in the brain. I've seen Pt brain scans of people addicted to cocaine side by side with people addicted to gambling. The same parts of the brain are lit up just as bright. In fact, anticipating the use of cocaine or gambling lights up the brain almost as much. We experience this all the time. The anticipation of a trip can be as joyful as the trip itself. Seeing your favorite band in concert sometimes doesn't match the joyful anticipation through the weeks since the tickets were purchased. Being scheduled to play in a sporting event can foment the same juicy expectation.

The neurotransmitter responsible for lighting up the brain is dopamine – the pleasure or reward neurotransmitter. Some call it the brain's happy juice. It's what flows when you watch a beautiful sunset. Dopamine floods the brain when powerful stimulants like cocaine and meth are used. Unfortunately, those drugs also damage the re-uptake of dopamine and eventually deplete it. When dopamine is finished, it's hard to enjoy that sunset.

The action you choose to trigger the happy juice matters. Drugs deplete dopamine levels in the brain. Naturally pleasurable activities don't. After enjoying a sunset, the brain has a natural re-uptake process for its dopamine. That's why you'll enjoy watching tomorrow's sunset too.

The best part is that exercise boosts levels of dopamine naturally. The healthiest mood-altering we can undertake is natural. Training is better than drugs. Watching a sunset or playing music is better than watching TV or gaming. Curling is better than sitting on the couch, eating Oreo cookies. Not that there isn't a time for eating cookies on the couch.

Endorphins create an energized euphoric feeling. It's the stuff that's responsible for "runner's high." The same effect can happen anytime you engage in prolonged strenuous exercise. Endorphins help curlers get through the large number of games demanded by some events. Endorphins are a natural pain reliever. They inhibit pain signals. That can explain why it seems we don't feel the effects of all those games until the event comes to a sudden end, and the juices stop flowing.

Epinephrine is what increases our heart rate and

breathing. It gives our muscles a jolt of energy, especially when we're triggered by fear. Too much of it can be paralyzing.

Cortisol is nature's built-in alarm. It's what activates the fight or flight response we have when threatened. When we're on high alert, it can shut other brain systems down to refocus resources on the impending fight. If we have too much cortisol running through us in a curling game, we're less likely to be able to process rational thought. The instinct is to run.

I think that's the appeal of watching scary movies. When you're fully immersed in a film like that, you feel what the character in the movie would feel. Cortisol triggers fight or flight. Epinephrine gives you a jolt, so you're ready to fight the bad guy. But your brain is fooled. You're still just sitting on your couch when the movie ends.

Curling requires the ability to control emotions and reason under stress, especially for skips. Front end players can release some of their stress with hard brushing. I've had a few what-was-I-thinking moments over the years. Afterward, when my brain systems returned to their normal state, it was clear to see I'd made a tactical mistake. Stress overrode conscious thought.

Sometimes when watching a scary movie, the suspense is too much. It becomes so unbearable you just want it to be over. Either the hero gets killed, escapes, or kills the attacker. Anything, as long as it gets resolved, and you can be relieved of the stress of the moment.

Curlers can experience something similar. It's not like hockey, where you can skate or check harder to blow the epinephrine out of your system. In curling, you stand there patiently while your opponent throws. Then you need to make a careful and deliberate decision and gently deliver a rock that requires fingertip precision. If the game is perceived to be important enough, you're throwing this delicate shot with cortisol and epinephrine pulsing through your brain.

I've been in games where I couldn't wait for it to be over. The stress of a shot for shot game sometimes got to be too much. Usually, I managed to refocus on the game at hand. It was hardest to focus on games where we were ahead, and a championship was near. The mind wanted to start thinking about the outcome and celebrating. But until the game was over and the result certain, the stress of the game continued.

This unfamiliar level of stress is why I think it's rare for teams to win that next level event on the first try. It's unusual for a team to win their first provincial championship, WCT event, or Brier on their first try. Players need to train their brains to be calm in those situations. They have to manage their emotions. Mental rehearsal and the help of sport psychologists can help immensely.

I generally enjoyed the stress of a tight match; in the same way that some people like suspenseful movies. I tried to take it on as a challenge. If I was tense or feeling stressed, that was a signal that I was not in a state of flow, as described earlier. Feeling stress was my body and brain telling me I was distracted by something; another player, external stimuli, or unhelpful thoughts. Usually, the pressure comes from thinking too much about the outcome and not staying present in the moment.

In his book "The Power of Now," Eckhart Tolle states: "you can practice this by taking any routine activity that normally is a means to an end and give it your fullest attention, so that it becomes an end in itself." Quiet your mind of all distractions and give your next rock your full attention. You might just re-enter a state of flow.

Anthropologists say that friendship is about creating small scale bonded groups that act as a protection to life's stresses. Early in our evolution, forming a trusted friendship group helped protect us from predators. Covid-19 lockdowns have taught us our friends are as important as oxygen. During these lockdowns, if we are fortunate enough to have all our basic needs met, we still crave contact with other people.

Our brains are craving an injection of oxytocin, the feeling of well-being, and bonding with others. Laughing, singing, and storytelling in small groups are examples of activities that boost oxytocin.

The positive experience of being on a curling team that's going to a bonspiel starts with the pick up of the first player. Traveling together and team bonding activities not only make you better friends, but they also make you better teammates. If somebody struggles in a game, the team has his back. There's a trust that the team will weather the challenges.

Sweep!

Not all my most memorable experiences were wins. Sometimes, a simple curling game was a juiced-up experience because of many factors. We had a game like that in Yorkton, Saskatchewan.

We played the big guy from Saskatchewan just a few months after he played a highly entertaining Brier semi-final against bad hair day from Quebec. We were playing him in his home town, in front of his crowd. The Painted Hand Casino Bonspiel was one of Canada's biggest cash-spiels and eventually became a Grand Slam event. The novelty of a new WCT event coming to town draws enormous crowds in the early years. It happened everywhere.

We were fortunate to be the only team in Manitoba, from north of the Trans-Canada, to get an invitation. In the glory days, invitations to the biggest bonspiels were highly coveted and hard to get. Each bonspiel determined who they would invite. Receiving an invitation was like getting your pro card, giving you access to the biggest prize money and the best teams in Canada.

In Yorkton, the field consisted of the who's who of Canadian curling. Games were played in the arena and adjoining curling club. They took two sheets of ice out of play in the curling club and installed bleachers from end to end. We played the big guy on a sheet right next to the sold-out bleachers.

The game was an epic battle from the beginning, well played, neither side giving an inch. The bleachers were installed right next to the sheet with none of the hockey board, plexiglass, or distance barriers between the crowd and players. Being so close, the crowd could hear the strategy discussions, not unlike hearing players mic'd up on TV.

I stood on the edge of the sheet when the other team threw. I was only an arm's length away from the first row of spectators and could hear their commentary on the game. Despite the fact I was as close as I was, people spoke as if I couldn't hear them. This fly-on-the-wall experience was very entertaining. I was tempted to turn around and give my input but didn't want to blow my cover.

The game continued to go back and forth. I felt so lucky to be in a match like that. We were the out-of-town team, the bad guys. Nobody in that building was cheering for us, but it was a knowledgeable crowd. I heard respect for us.

I decide to shed my invisibility late in the game. Some of the crowd were wondering what our opponent was planning. I turned around and said, "They're looking at playing the raise." They looked as if a player on their TV had turned and spoken directly to them through the screen. That section suddenly realized I'd heard everything they said the whole game. I smiled and slid away.

The game was too good to be settled in ten ends. We got a rock covered behind a guard in the extra end. The big guy needed the four foot for the win. He slid out and let go of the stone. He was light. His sweepers jumped it instantly. They put their heads down and pounded it with all their might. The rock was barely moving – no way, I thought.

Powerful sweeping warms the ice and creates a thin film, reducing the friction between the rock and ice surface, like a plastic cup gliding on spilled milk. The big guy's sweepers weren't slowing down. They had their entire body weight over the brush head, moving it vigorously back and forth while propelling themselves with their feet. I can't think of a sport equivalent for the task of brushing; it's like shoveling concrete as fast as you can while dancing.

The rock was barely moving when it entered the house. The crowd had been cheering the whole way; the Saskatchewan thirteenth man (fifth man in this case) urged the sweepers to find everything they had. The rock crept into the top four foot – one inch better than ours, and the crowd erupted.

The sweepers still couldn't catch their breath enough to speak when I shook their hands.

The Ice Man

Some of the biggest bonspiels in Canada reserved

between one and four spots for the less famous teams. All the top guns got direct entry. The rest of us would fight it out in a qualifying bonspiel- curling's equivalent to Q-school.

One memorable year we won a spot into what was then known as The Coke Classic, played at the Assiniboine Memorial Club in Winnipeg. The qualifying spiel had gone well for us. We'd strung a few wins together and clinched our spot against a former Brier runner-up.

The main event included everybody who was anybody and us. We were still going strong on Saturday and had the evening off. Our next game wouldn't be until Sunday morning against The Ice Man. We decided to get out of the rink for the evening and watch a football game. We got tickets to watch the Bombers play the Argos.

I felt a little chill near half time. Then I started shivering and couldn't stop. I shivered all night, and my body started to ache. I had the flu. I felt terrible, but there was no way I was going to sit out a game against one of my curling idols. Getting a match up like that was the very reason I played the game at all.

In my daydreams, I play world champions fearlessly. I visualize myself confidently calling and making the most complicated of shots. I see myself ready, willing, and able to win.

On this day, I was sick as a dog. I gave it a valiant effort and wished I could have been at my best, but I wasn't. Something I often got when playing one of the best was a glimpse into their decision-making process for selecting shots. Most of the time, the obvious shot is the correct call. But not always.

We had the hammer in a messy end. They had two counters in the twelve-foot, and there was junk all over the front. When they came to throw their last rock, there was a three-foot-wide port that included the centerline. Most people would quickly choose to draw through the port and put a better counter into the four foot. That would leave me with a draw through the same port to try to better his shot and score a point.

They looked at the situation for a moment and had a discussion. They had only the two rocks in the twelve-foot; usually, that's not good enough to steal. But they realized that dropping a guard into the port would cut me off from any direct path to the house. It was brilliant. All I had left was an angle raise on a heavier, more unpredictable outside path. I guessed wrong and missed.

The Ice Man, with his two world championships, is known for being the purest rock thrower in the game. He's also known as an enthusiastic partier and one of the nicest people in the game. When we shook hands to concede, he cut me slack by saying how tricky the outside parts of the sheets were. He said he lost a game the same way the day before. There was no need for him to be as kind as he was; I was nobody. He was gracious anyway.

There was a moment in that game where I paused

and looked around. On the sheet next to us, The Wrench was playing another world champion. Two former Brier teams played on the other side. We were in the middle, locked in a battle with The Ice Man. It was a pinch-me moment.

Later that day, we went upstairs to grab a sandwich before the next game. A former world champion was on his eighth or ninth rum and coke, having been eliminated from the bonspiel. He said, "Those rocks are like snowflakes. Every one is different." He shook his head, "If they don't fix that, this club has a future as a bingo hall."

He was out, and we were going back onto the ice.

Cowboys

The Canadian Cattleman's Championship was an annual competition hosted in turns by various provinces. Competitors needed to be connected to the industry in some way. The event attracted tough men from feedlots, auctions, the trucking industry, cattle buyers, and a few primary producers.

A few people from my area attended regularly. I'd been asked to come along several times but couldn't make it happen due to conflicts with other competitions and my reluctance to join the excesses that went with the Cattleman's. Stories coming back from these events could curl your hair.

I held a cup of coffee and listened while a fellow cattleman made his pitch to have me join his team.

He said the total take from the calcutta was in the mid-six figures. He assured me that they had a limit on what they'd pay for their own team, never more than twenty grand. I made it look like the catch in my throat was due to the hot coffee.

He went on to say that a team from Alberta had brought in a ringer, and it would be an excellent strategy to throw the first game and make a run in the second event. Payouts were given only to the finalists in each event, and there were always tough matchups in the semis. I rarely gambled more than the three loonies needed to play dice, and I'd never thrown a curling game in my life. I decided to take a pass.

Years later, I had to see for myself. The participant registration packages included a new broom and more drink tickets than one should use in a month- never mind a weekend. The opening banquet featured large barbequed steaks with all the trimmings. Men with no necks gobbled steak and beer in the shade of their tractor caps. Other men reflected fluorescent light from their foreheads. One forehead succumbed to gravity and spent the evening swimming in gravy.

A cattle auctioneer announced the beginning of the calcutta. The industry had taken a hit from BSE. This event wasn't what it once was, but the fact remained, the people in the room were comfortable with big money and risk. They filled multi-million dollar feedlot orders and watched markets go up or down. They'd seen extreme weather events destroy feed crops and a strange disease close international borders.

There was no shortage of booze and bravado to fuel the bidding. Every day, they sat around a ring and looked each other in the eye while bidding on pens of cattle. Bidding on drunk curlers gave no one any pause.

We managed to buy our own team. We were bid up a little by a cattle buyer from Manitoba who knew me. We decided to give him a cut. After the calcutta was over, the gambling continued in the back rooms. That's where the big money went. It was not for anybody on my team.

All the food and drink were provided by various sponsors all weekend. The Saturday banquet featured monstrous portions of prime rib. On the ice, we got off to a good start. We won a couple of games against decent enough teams, but certainly, squads that we should beat. Tough hard-living cattlemen don't concede anything readily, so we had to play hard. Everybody expected to win, and nobody took losing particularly well.

We played a team from Guelph, Ontario, in the semifinal. They had won this event in a previous year. It seemed to shock them to lose to us. It set up a final against a foursome from Alberta that played together competitively in road-to-the Brier men's play-downs. We were over-matched but held our own in a surprisingly well-played game. The difference came down to a couple of small mistakes from our team. It was a good game and a fitting final.

And by making the first event's finals, we qualified for prize money and a hefty calcutta payout. I went home with more money from this than I had from qualifying in World Curling Tour events. Maybe I was wrong about the Cattleman's.

The Big Win

I reached a point in my curling career where it seemed like every game I played got reported on the radio. There were between one and three teams from the Parkland that did any touring, and CKDM did a good job of reporting our results back to its listeners.

We were in Grand Forks, North Dakota, and drawn against one of those famous curling household names. They didn't make it to Grand Forks in time for their game with us for some unknown reason. We won by default.

Volunteers at World Curling Tour events uploaded results onto the WCT website. The media used that website to source results. Defaults were always recorded as a score of ten to nothing, but there was nothing to indicate the game was a default. The radio station reported that we'd beaten this big-name team by a score of ten to nothing. The report ran on every sportscast, on the hour, all day. The most lopsided victory ever attributed to me – never actually happened.

IN THE TWILIGHT

"We don't stop playing because we grow old,
we grow old because we stop playing."
George Bernard Shaw

On the eve of my sixtieth birthday, I did the math. It's been fifty years since I played my first game of curling with my grade six class. That's half a century! I've played somewhere between twenty-five hundred and three thousand games since then; I've likely thrown upwards of twenty thousand practice rocks. I've slid the equivalent of six hundred and eighty miles...on my toe. That explains some of the aches in the knees.

An inventory of the crests in a cigar box reveals that there have been ten trips to the Provincial Men's Championships. There were a few mixed provincials and a couple of seniors' events as well. There were appearances in the Manitoba Curling Tour Championships, some super league titles, and all-star selections. Fifty years of curling in a cigar box.

There was a period of time when my teams regularly ranked among the World Curling Tour top 100; the highest, a ranking of number thirty-seven. I never accepted that as our real standing in the world. I live in Manitoba, where numerous WCT events were a short drive away. It's like fishing in a lake with tons of fish. One could get the impression you're better at fishing than you are.

I was fortunate to grow up in a community that satisfied its craving for competition and social interaction at the curling rink. I began my competitive career when the legends of the sixties and seventies were still active. What an honor it was to play them. I played through a time that saw the introduction of revolutionary rule changes, sharp rocks, and the World Curling Tour.

I've beaten Olympic medalists, provincial, national, and world champions. And I've lost to knee sliders and drunks. I played in an era where it was easily possible to play knee sliders, drunks, and world champions all in the same week.

I've learned a few lessons along the way: curling lessons, life lessons, and maybe a bit of self-awareness. Curling can be a humbling game. No matter how high you fly, you can't stay there forever. My local reputation has given me a few wins against opponents who don't know how fragile my advantages over them were. If they knew, they'd have relaxed and beat me more often. I suspect teams above mine know this secret too. When you've got the best team in the region, you're like the tough guy on a hockey team. You need your opponent to fear a thrashing, but you don't want to take one yourself and bust the myth.

Your psyche needs to walk the tight rope of confidence and self-delusion. A misstep can cause a crash. Confidence is desirable, but bravado will cause a hard fall. Weak will forces the tightrope to shake and wobble. Unwavering volition can carry you far. You want to be "in the zone," but you can't fight your way in. You have to be given access to the right state of mind.

From the time I first discovered the state of *flow*, I wanted to be in that frame of mind for every game. I found that that wasn't possible. It took work to get there. It was during the periods when I practiced and played the most that I more easily entered the desired state of mind. Preparation produces confidence. Through repetition, and over-learning the movements of a delivery, confidence grows. If I could throw practice rock after practice rock perfectly, I thought I could duplicate the same mechanics in a game.

Physically throwing rocks wasn't always possible to the degree I wanted. Visualization had to fill the void. It takes a lot of psychic energy to visualize and feel the release of a stone in your mind. You still need to find time for it. When I was at work or on the floor with my kids, I wanted to be present, in-the-moment, so I chose not to be thinking about the game at those times. There were times I went into important games, knowing I wasn't prepared physically. I hadn't played or practiced enough. I tried to compensate by getting to the right place in my mind. Sometimes this caused me to be edgy or too amped up.

One year, I decided to put up my Christmas lights a couple of days before zone play-downs. I was already playing the competition in my mind. To install the lights, I had bought a new style of a tab that you could slide under the shingle instead of stapling the string to the house. I put the tabs on all the strings and placed them over the peak and down the other side. I was just a few feet from the end when I accidentally let go of the end of the string, causing the first light to pull the tab out from the shingle. Then the next one pulled out, and then all of them popped out, one after another, like falling dominoes. I'm not proud of the reaction that followed. Once I cooled down, I thought if that's the state of mind I need to be in to play well, forget it. I don't want to be that person off the ice. But it was a dilemma. When the weekend arrived, I was ready for the competition. I had found the state of flow, and we won. It was clearly important to do something to prepare for an event without letting it consume me. For me, it was a pre-event neurosis. I'd once read, "Life is hard. You can accept that or become neurotic." I fluctuated between self-defeating thoughts and cockiness, looking for the needle to settle in the psychological sweet spot.

I knew an outstanding curler who needed to throw up before every game. I knew I was ready when I... ahem, eliminated three times before the first game of an event. It was nature's enema, ensuring that when the fight began, I wouldn't shit my pants.

My supervisor asked me to give a presentation to my co-workers when I was a young employee at BMHC. I went into it overconfident, complacent, and unprepared. I'd done public speaking in 4-H and was good at it. In my mind – I got this.

I got really nervous just before the presentation. I knew my material but hadn't rehearsed the delivery. I stumbled and stammered through. My co-workers asked helpful questions to get me on track. I had a deer-in-the-headlights look. I hadn't anticipated questions. My neck got hot, and my face flushed. My audience wore pained expressions of sympathy. It was a disaster.

I've been called upon to speak many times since then, and I've tried very hard to avoid a similar collapse. I prepared by knowing my material inside and out, constructing and rehearsing the sentences I'd use, and anticipating every possible question. In my professional life, I've done countless public presentations. I've also made speeches at political fundraisers, done eulogies, and spoken at conferences. I get butterflies every time and usually need to eliminate just once more, but I've managed to avoid the full-on collapse I experienced all those years ago.

I've done the same thing with curling. Just as with speaking, I've gone into games overconfident, complacent, and unprepared. Just because I've thrown a gazillion out-turn hits in my life doesn't mean I can sleep through the next one. Just because I know how to read ice doesn't mean I shouldn't continue to watch carefully for changing conditions and remain alert.

Sometimes it's hard to understand why a team isn't performing. Everybody seems to be doing the right things, but the results don't follow. I liken it to playing in a band. I play with a group of guys just for fun and occasionally in public. There are days when everybody is playing the right notes, but there's nothing special about it. And then there are days when we're in sync with each other. We're not just playing notes; we're making music.

A curling team can experience something similar. When the unit is in sync, it's more than four guys making shots. The four people become a single entity that is more potent than the sum of its parts.

I ruminate about the possibility that I've played most of my career in the wrong position. It may be that I was better suited to playing third. Or maybe, I didn't fully embrace the role of the skip. I started as a skip in grade school because I was the most enthusiastic about the game. I knew the difference between in-turns and out-turns. I wanted to throw last. I've always loved throwing the last rock. I wanted to have the hammer in my hand when the game was on the line. I rarely felt nervous in those situations. I liked having control of the game. I would be the one to determine how we would approach an end and what strategy we used. I really enjoyed playing the position of skip. I didn't always embrace the managing-the-game part.

I was a riverboat gambler when the best strategy was to blank the next three ends. I had some lineups that were often over-matched A better game-winning strategy, when over-matched, is to keep things simple, keep the score close, and wait for a mistake from the other team. It may be true that defense wins championships, but I found that style boring and under-stimulating. I forced things when I shouldn't have because I wanted action more than I wished for a two to one win.

If you play football, there will be a coaching staff to review your play, teach proper technique, and address your mistakes. In curling, that role falls upon the skip. I didn't do that very well. I've seen the guy playing in a small community bonspiel for small donated prizes, and he's giving his team shit for missing. Who wants to be that guy? But if you're on a team with aspirations, how do you improve if problems aren't addressed? The same mistakes get repeatedly made because it's hard to correct or advise a teammate when you're not in the more detached role of coach. It's not always well received. To understate it, some grown men have large and fragile egos.

I played the position of third a few times over the years. It might have been the right position for my temperament, psyche, and skill set. I wasn't a killer. I loved to compete and perform well and certainly chased the feeling of a victory. But a criticism I've had is, sometimes it didn't look like I wanted it enough. I once played match play golf with a guy I barely knew. He said, "You're a decent enough golfer, but you're too nice a guy to win anything." It is true that I generally have an easy-going disposition and don't often get too worked up. I also know that I perform best when I'm in my "happy place," a state of calm quiet. But when easy-going isn't working, it can look like indifference or complacency. Maybe sometimes it was.

I may have had a higher ceiling as a third. I always found it an adjustment to move to this position. As a skip, I chose my own shot and had the time it took to get to the other end, to prepare mentally to throw. As a third, I had to get my head around the shot called for me and be ready to throw sooner. When I got into this new rhythm, it was good. I could add value to the team by making a good set-up shot. The role of the third can also include being a liaison between the front end and skip. I'm a decent communicator and should have been better at doing that job. Most importantly, a third should say the right things at the right time to the skip. The skip carries the weight of the game, and a good third knows how to support that, like a good vice president.

I played third for four or five high functioning skips. They all needed a different kind of support based on their personalities and approaches to the game. With some, presenting another shot option should be done delicately. Some required more talking through the thinking, and some less.

I had a curious communication style with one

person in particular. For the first four years we played together, I skipped. The next four, he skipped. We had some success lined up either way. Our communication was the same with either line up too – next to none. It might have been because we were on the same page most of the time, both knew what shot needed to be called, and both knew what had just happened. There was nothing more to say. In a typical end, the skip would say, "I'm thinking hack weight. Broom about here." The third would say, "Looks good." After the shot was made, the skip would stand right next to the third, and no words would be spoken. None needed. If the shot was missed, the skip would stand beside the third with arms folded. After a minute or so, he might ask, "Too much weight?" The third would nod almost imperceptibly. Another fifteen minutes might pass before anything more was said.

People watching us often thought we were mad at each other. In reality, there were few people I got along with as well as I did with him. This austere style of communication was our mode of operation for eight years. It's not a style I recommend. We, ourselves, acknowledged that we'd have been well served to communicate a bit more. Off the ice, we'd both be considered quite outgoing. On the ice, it was all business.

I should have played third more often with skips who were better game managers than I. I should have played more with skips who played by the book. I knew the book and ignored it too often. I played with some excellent game managers and last rock throwers; I had success with them. Early in my career, I should have redefined myself as the kind of third you want on your team. The truth is, I'd get itchy. I craved the rush of throwing the last rock again. I couldn't shake it.

If Christopher Lloyd and Michael J Fox ever pick me up in a DeLorean, these are the lessons I'll take back for the redo. I'll be dangerous. If I've accumulated any wisdom over the years, it's because I've tried to live my life fully, not necessarily because I got any of it right.

The Buffalo

My last story is saved for the end, not because it's any sort of crowning achievement; it just happens to be the last competitive event I played. Our team qualified for the Canada 55+ Games by winning a provincial playoff. The games were held in the month of August in Saint John, New Brunswick.

I finally had my buffalo. It's a bison, more accurately, contained in Manitoba's provincial crest. I'd dreamed of wearing the buffalo in a Brier. That didn't happen. I'd be wearing it at an event where all the participants were over the age of fifty-five. I was no less grateful to be carrying provincial colors. I'm sure people from other provinces are proud to wear their colors too. But in Manitoba, the curling heartland, the buffalo is worn with pride and the weight of expectation. Manitoba expects its representatives to challenge for the championship at every level. It wasn't the Brier, but we were happy to carry "the weight of the buffalo."

The Canada 55+ Games were quite a spectacle. There were numerous events like track and field, swimming, pickleball, tennis, slow pitch, golf, hockey, and our sport, curling. There were upwards of five thousand older adult athletes from all over Canada. What a testament to healthy, active living. There were so many people whose appearances defied their age.

The weather was mild this August in Saint John. We took advantage of that by sampling the great restaurants on the waterfront and exploring the city.

We got off to a good start by winning our first game. We were a bit nervous about it because nobody had had an opportunity to throw practice rocks since the spring. All we had was a pre-event practice session the day before the event began.

The other competitors were great. These were all competitive people who'd played in some higher-level stuff when they were younger, just like us. But nobody had any illusions about what this competition was. It was for people over fifty-five who were still *able* to curl. That said, the games were quite well played.

After games, we'd join the other team around a table with a pitcher of beer, Pepsi, or coffee. Some people are still curling at this age because they've switched from beer. We'd exchange curling war stories. We'd listen to descriptions of other parts of the country, past careers, and good jokes. Sometimes, we'd discover we knew some of the same people.

We were Manitobans, and we were tuckers, sliding up on our toes. We could still bring the heat, and soon word spread that you shouldn't get behind on the scoreboard against Manitoba. They'll just run everything after that. It was great fun.

Consecutive wins against Saskatchewan, Alberta, and Ontario put us in the gold medal game against Nova Scotia. It was an excellent game. They got a bit of momentum when we guarded a favorable situation but still gave up two when they played a raise that worked out better than the call. We had trouble getting ends set up after that, and they could smell victory.

In the end, we came up short. It would be a silver medal around our necks, not gold. It doesn't matter to the story that we thought we were the better team. It doesn't matter how many times out of ten we would typically beat them. On that day, they were better. They won fair and square.

The silver medal might be the most fitting end to my competitive curling career if that remains my last game. It's symbolic of how all the rest of it went; pretty good, but short of my potential. I can live with that. Playing up to my potential would have required more games, more practice, more sacrifices. And still, no guarantee that I'd achieve anything more.

If playing to my full potential meant giving up more

of the things I did when I wasn't curling – no deal. The other stuff was always more important. If it were possible to correlate effort with results objectively, I probably got all the results I deserved. How could I expect more without committing further? I'm grateful. I'm a farm boy who grew up loving curling, and I got a chance to peek behind the curtain of the high-level competitive game. Curling enriched my life. I couldn't reasonably ask for more.

About three weeks after our return from that terrific trip to Saint John, we gathered at my place. We sat around picnic tables under oak trees on a mild September afternoon. The leaves were starting to fade and give way to fall colors. The lake was a bold shade of blue that day. We had a barbeque supper together; Ray and Lisa, Dwight and Jamie, Keith and Donna, Brenda and I.

We took turns going for a steam in my recently built outdoor cedar sauna. Keith brought a bottle of newly discovered rum. "You won't believe how smooth it is," he said.

We drank a toast to our silver medals. We laughed. We talked about how things are... and about how things used to be.

Bibliography

Cherry, *How Reinforcement Schedules Work:* Verywellmind.com. 2020

Csikszentmihalyi, *Flow: The Psychology of Optimal Experience:* Harper and Row. 1990

Doidge, *The Brain That Changes Itself:* Penguin Books. 2007

Grassie, *Kings of the Rings: 125 Years of the World's Biggest Bonspiel.* Great Plains Publications. 2012

Hackner, Lukowich, Lang, *Curling to Win:* McGraw-Hill Ryerson. 1987

Harari, *Sapiens: A Brief History of Humankind:* Dvir Publishing House. Harper. 2011

Lukowich, Folk, Gowsell, *The Curling Book: With Tips For Beginners and Experts.* Western Producer Prairie Books. 1981

Mott, Allardyce, *Curling Capital: Winnipeg and the Roarin' Game, 1876 to 1988:* The University of Manitoba Press. 1989

Murray, *The Curling Companion:* Collins Publishing. 1981

Rosenberg, Feder, *Behavioral Addictions: Criteria, Evidence, and Treatment:* Academic Press. 2014

Scholz, Bernard, *Between the Sheets: The Silver Lining:* Polished Publishing Group. 2011

Spino, *Breakthrough: Maximum Sports Training:* Pocket Books, Simon and Shuster Inc. 1984

Tolle, *The Power of Now:* Namaste Publishing. 1999

Tutko, Tosi, *Sports Psyching: Playing Your Best Game All of the Time:* Tarcher Press. 1976

Watson, *Ken Watson on Curling,* The Copp Clark Co. Ltd. 1950

Weeks, *The Brier: The History of Canada's Most Celebrated Curling Championship.* MacMillan Canada. 1995

Wiecek, *Choosing Cash Over Glory:* Winnipeg Free Press. Jan 23, 1999

ACKNOWLEDGEMENT

Thank you Brenda, Jennifer, Graham, Dale, Jean, Bob, Marc, Resby, Kathy, and Karen.

All of you know the ways you've contributed to this project - and so do I. I appreciate it very much.

raekujanpaa55@gmail.com

Made in the USA
Monee, IL
26 March 2021